ATV
Trails Guide
Moab, UT

By CHARLES A. WELLS

Author on Top of the World, Trail #21.

Photo by Neal Swisher

Easy • Moderate • Difficult
ATV Riding Adventures

FunTreks, Inc.

1

Published by FunTreks, Inc.
P. O. Box 3127, Monument, CO 80132-3127
Phone: Toll Free 877-222-7623, Fax: 719-277-7411
E-mail: books@funtreks.com
Web site: www.funtreks.com

Edited by Shelley Mayer
Cover design, photography, maps, and production by Charles A. Wells

First Edition

Library of Congress Control Number 2005939139
ISBN 0-9664976-7-8

Printed in China.

To order additional books, call toll-free 1-877-222-7623 or use order form in back of
this book. You may also order online at www.funtreks.com.

TRAIL UPDATES:
For latest trail updates and changes, check the *Trails Updates* page on our Web site at
www.funtreks.com.

GUARANTEE OF SATISFACTION:
If you are dissatisfied with this book in any way, regardless of where you bought it,
please call our toll-free number during business hours at 1-877-222-7623. We promise
to do whatever it takes to make you happy.

DISCLAIMER

Travel in Utah's backcountry is, by its very nature, potentially dangerous
and could result in property damage, injury, or even death. The scope of
this book cannot predict every possible hazard you may encounter. If you
ride any of the trails in this book, you acknowledge these risks and assume
full responsibility. You are the final judge as to whether a trail is safe to
ride on any given day, whether your vehicle is capable of the journey and
what supplies you should carry. The information contained herein cannot
replace good judgment and proper preparation on your part. The publisher
and author of this book disclaim any and all liability for bodily injury,
death, or property damage that could occur to you or any fellow travelers.

ACKNOWLEDGMENTS

My sincere thanks to the following individuals and organizations who helped with this book:

Canyonlands Natural History Association. Cindy Hardgrave, Director, brought to my attention the need for a quality Moab ATV guide and helped get things started. Thanks also to CNHA's Peggy McNeal, Julie McKinnon and Nancy Kosa, who provided helpful advice and local contact information.

The Bureau of Land Management in Moab, Manti-La Sal National Forest in Monticello, Grand County Road Department, Sand Flats Recreation Area and the Utah State Parks OHV Education Office. Hard-working staffers helped with trail selection, made suggestions for improvements and helped with proofing.

Neal Swisher, a 43-year resident of Moab and an ardent rider of ATVs. Over the years, he has worn out a half dozen ATVs covering more than 50,000 miles in Moab's backcountry. For more than two decades, starting in the 1960s, he was a "Catskinner" (bulldozer operator) building roads for oil exploration. His knowledge of Moab's ATV trails is unsurpassed. Today, at the age of 73, Neal still rides nearly every day. He tirelessly guided me on many trails in this book, including several lesser-known routes. (See Neal on his yellow Suzuki King Quad throughout this book.)

Hans Weibel and wife Madeleine, 28-year residents of Moab and avid ATV riders. Hans shared his diverse knowledge of Moab's history based on years of riding and hiking the area. His input helped add local flavor to the book. Hans and Madeleine frequently took time from their busy schedules to show me their favorite trails. Hans also proofed the book and made helpful suggestions.

Dale Parriott of *ridewithrespect.org*, impassioned local dirt biker, is responsible for establishing many single-track trails in the area, including the Sovereign Trail System.

Kyle Carlisle, Bob and Paul Kirkpatrick of the Pathfinderzz ATV Club in Provo, UT; Joe Lyman, Mike Washburn and Bob Turri of the San Juan County ATV Club; Ethan Remington and Jason Schmidt of Washington Adventure Quads; Scott McFarland of Highpoint Hummer & ATV Tours; Fred Hink of Arrowhead Motorsports; Brad Franklin; Michael Scully and Scott Morrison. Special thanks to Jody Biershied who loaned me an ATV for a few days and Mark McDonald who pulled my ATV from the mud in Kane Creek Canyon.

Shelley Mayer, for her thorough editing of this book, Joan Aaland, who keeps our office running smoothly, Marcia LeVault, for her many hours of hard work, and my wife, Beverly, for her encouragement.

Kane Creek Canyon Rim, Trail #18.

CONTENTS

Trail List

*Author's Favorites

Trail Locator Map

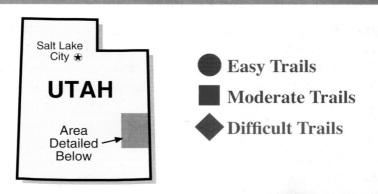

Easy Trails

Moderate Trails

Difficult Trails

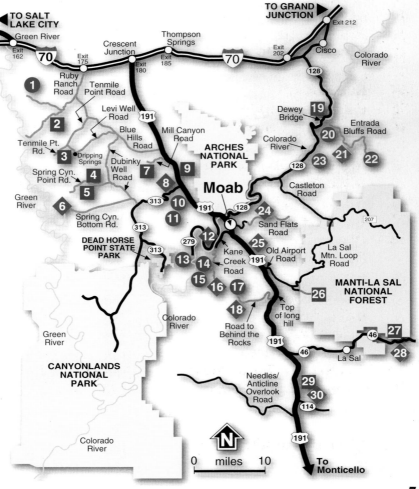

Trails Listed by Difficulty

Although trails are grouped into three major categories, there are still differences in difficulty within each group. For example, Potash Road is easier than Pole Canyon Rim even though both are rated easy. Trails are progressively more difficult as you pan down the list, although you may have to skip several trails to see any significant difference.

No.	Trail	Page	Rating
13.	Potash Road	80	Easy
23.	Onion Creek	120	Easy
22.	Dolores River Overlook	116	Easy
10.	Gemini Bridges	68	Easy
14.	Hurrah Pass	84	Easy
17.	Picture Frame Arch	96	Easy
15.	Chicken Corners	88	Easy
11.	Bull Canyon	72	Easy
1.	Crystal Geyser	32	Easy
20.	Pole Canyon Rim	108	Easy
2.	White Wash Sand Dunes	36	Moderate
27.	Hideout Mesa	136	Moderate
7.	Determination Towers	56	Moderate
5.	Dellenbaugh Tunnel, Secret Spire	48	Moderate
3.	Tenmile Wash	40	Moderate
29.	Cameo Cliffs/ Wilson Arch	144	Moderate
9.	Sovereign Trail	64	Moderate
26.	La Sal Pass	132	Moderate
4.	Rainbow Terrace	44	Moderate
19.	Dome Plateau	104	Moderate
8.	Sevenmile Rim	60	Difficult
6.	Hey Joe Canyon	52	Difficult
21.	Top of the World	112	Difficult
30.	Cameo Cliffs/ El Diablo	148	Difficult
18.	Kane Creek Canyon Rim	100	Difficult
24.	Fins & Things	124	Difficult
25.	Steelbender Loop	128	Difficult
16.	Kane Creek Canyon	92	Difficult
28.	Greasewood Canyon	140	Difficult
12.	Poison Spider Mesa	76	Difficult

Trail Ratings Defined

Trail ratings are very subjective. Conditions change for many reasons, including weather and time of year. An easy trail can quickly become difficult when washed out by a rainstorm or blocked by a fallen rock. You must be the final judge of a trail's condition on the day you ride it. If any part of a trail is difficult, the entire trail is rated difficult. You may be able to ride a significant portion of a trail before reaching the difficult spot. Read each trail description carefully for specific information. Turn around when in doubt. Always wear a helmet.

● Easy Trails

Gravel, dirt, clay, sand, or mildly rocky trail or road. Gentle grades. Water levels low except during periods of heavy runoff. Adequate room to pass. Where shelf conditions exist, trail is wide and well maintained with minor sideways tilt. Most trails are passable when wet; however, certain types of clay can become impassable under wet conditions. Smaller, two-wheel-drive ATVs are usually adequate in good weather. Easy trails are best suited for novice riders.

■ Moderate Trails

Rougher and rockier surfaces require slower running speeds. Some riding experience is needed for steeper climbs and descents. Rock-stacking may be necessary to get over the worst spots. Considerable weight shifting may be necessary to offset sideways tilt. Mud can be deep and you may get stuck. Certain types of clay can become impassable when wet. Sand can be soft and steep. Water may be too deep for smaller ATVs. Larger ATVs can usually get through except during periods of heavy runoff. Aggressive tires needed for two-wheel-drive machines. Four-wheel-drive is usually best.

◆ Difficult Trails

Very rough and rocky surfaces require careful tire placement. Slopes may be extremely steep with scary sideways tilt. Skillful riding is necessary to avoid tipping or flipping over. Rock-stacking may be necessary in places, and the worst spots could require assistance from other people. Sand can be very soft and steep. Shelf roads can be very narrow with daunting cliffs. Water and mud can be very deep. Wet clay surfaces can be impassable. Some powerful two-wheel-drive ATVs may get through under good weather conditions, but four-wheel-drive with low-range gearing is highly recommended.

Fins & Things, Trail #24.

INTRODUCTION

Few OHV experiences can rival the fun of riding an ATV in Moab's backcountry. An endless variety of undulating and challenging terrain combined with spectacular scenery provide an unforgettable experience. Perhaps you've heard of Moab's "slickrock" and wondered why people come from all over the world to experience it. The name "slickrock" is misleading. It is a carryover from a time when wooden wagon wheels clattered and slid across the hard rock. Today's modern rubber tires, however, provide super traction. This enables ATVs to climb and descend unbelievably steep inclines. Riding up and down these slopes requires some practice, even for experienced riders. Not everyone will have the strength or desire to try it. Each rider must evaluate the steepness and proceed based on his own skills. (To help with your decision, see "RIDING ON SLICKROCK," page 25.)

Before heading into the backcountry, it's critical that you understand the importance of staying on existing trails. Leaving the trail causes unnecessary erosion, kills vegetation and spoils the beauty of the land. Also important is proper trail etiquette. You'll be sharing the trails with hikers, mountain bikers, horseback riders, pets and pack animals. You'll need to do everything possible to minimize disturbances created by your speed, noise and dust. (Read more on pages 20-25.)

Don't let Moab's beauty fool you. It can be a dangerous place for the foolish and ill-prepared. Temperatures can be extreme, both hot and cold. You may be parched one minute and soaked to the skin the next. In addition, it is very easy to get lost, so make sure you carry a topographic map. The maps in this book are intended to help with directions only. You'll want more information if you become disoriented. Don't rely strictly on a GPS unit. You could drop it on a rock or batteries could go dead. (See "ROUTE FINDING TIPS," page 26.)

USING THIS BOOK

Each trail in this book has a photo page, a general information page, a directions page and a map page. Read each page carefully before you head out.

The photo page is intended to show you actual trail conditions, not just scenery. Photos include both positive and negative aspects of a trail. A sample of the most difficult spot is usually included. Often photos make the trail look easier than it is. For example, photos of steep spots seldom look as steep as they really are.

The general information page provides directions to the start of the trail, where to unload and camp, difficulty details, highlights, time requirements, length of trail, a basic trail description, other routes nearby and services.

The directions page and map page work together as one. When the map is turned sideways, so are the directions. The two pages together can be copied (for personal use only) on one 8-1/2″ x 11″ sheet of paper and carried in your pocket while on the trail. The main route, described in the directions, is shown in green, blue or red depending on the difficulty level. This route has a shadow to help it stand out on the page. Other routes nearby are shown in light brown and are not described in the directions. Waypoints for the main route are shown on the directions page while waypoints for other routes are shown on the map. A blended gray tone is used to show deep canyons and tall cliffs. Mileage is shown with an overall grid. Check the scale at the bottom of the map because each scale is different.

All trails in this book were ridden and documented by the author. A few were done in the fall of 2004, but most were ridden in the spring of 2005. Directions were written from the author's personal notes and all maps were created using the author's own track logs.

THE RIGHT TRAIL FOR YOU

It is important to select a trail that matches your riding skills and your equipment. On page 9, you'll find a detailed description of each basic trail rating. Page 8 lists the trails in order of difficulty. Within each category, trails are listed with easiest at the top and hardest at the bottom. Remember that ratings are subjective and can change quickly because of weather and other unforeseen circumstances.

If you are a novice rider, start with the easiest trails at the top of the list on page 8. After mastering basic skills, move down the list. The toughest trails at the bottom are for advanced riders only. Not everyone can attain this level. Don't let others pressure you into riding a trail beyond your skill level. Challenge yourself in small increments. Make sure you read each trail description yourself. Don't rely on others to translate.

ATVs come in all shapes, sizes and horsepower levels. Easy trails can generally be ridden with smaller 2-wheel-drive machines. As trails become more difficult, additional horsepower, 4-wheel drive and low-range gearing become more important. Steep slickrock climbs require substantial horsepower. Small ATVs should not be used on trails like Kane Creek Canyon, Trail #16, where water crossings can be deep.

ABOUT MOAB

It's easy to find your way around the small town of Moab. Main Street (Highway 191) runs north and south all the way through town. Center Street and Main Street, where the Moab Information Center is located, marks the center of town. If you need lodging or camping, it's a good idea to call well in advance. Things fill up quickly on weekends and when frequent special events are underway (e.g., Easter Jeep Safari, 24 Hours of Moab Bike Race, etc). Up-to-date information is available on the Moab Travel Council Web site (www.discovermoab.com).

ATV rentals and servicing. There are several places in Moab to rent ATVs. (Check www.discovermoab.com/autorental.htm for latest information or just drive down Main Street.) These places may be able to help with minor service; however, you'll have to drive to Price, UT, or Grand Junction, CO, to find a major ATV dealer. (See appendix for contact information.)

Weather: Spring and fall are the best seasons to be in Moab. The average daytime temperatures range from 64 degrees in March to 84 in May. June through August average highs are near 100 degrees with maximum highs reaching 110 in July. September's average high temperature is in the mid 80s while October is perfect at 77 degrees. The wettest months are April, July, and October, with the worst month, October, averaging 1.6 inches of precipitation. When it rains, it can come all at once. Flash floods are a major concern in canyon country. Winter weather is often mild but days are short and it gets cold quickly after the sun goes down.

Town History: Moab experienced several boom-and-bust economic periods during the 20th century. The most significant was the uranium mining period during the 1950s. Following World War II, demand for uranium ore was high. The town quickly grew as mining operations shot up everywhere. Many of the OHV roads are remnants of these mining days. You can still see bulldozer tracks and rock cuts on many trails such as Poison Spider Mesa and Sevenmile Rim. In places, core drilling holes remain exposed in the slickrock. Demand for uranium died during the 1960s, spelling a near-disaster for the town. Many jobs were replaced by underground potash mining operations until 18 miners were killed in an underground explosion in 1964. The operation was quickly converted to automated solution mining, requiring far fewer workers.

Meanwhile, Hollywood discovered Moab's backcountry was a great place to shoot western movies. Over the years, dozens of movies have been shot in the area, including *Indiana Jones* in 1988, *Thelma and Louise* in 1990, and *Geronimo* in 1993.

Today, tourism is Moab's biggest industry, driven primarily by the establishment of two National Parks and the growing popularity of mountain biking and four-wheeling.

Arches National Monument was dedicated in 1929 and became a National Park in 1971, seven years after Canyonlands National Park.

The Slickrock Bike Trail started first as a motorcycle trail in 1969. Today it is predominantly used for mountain biking, but motorcyclists still use the trail. People come from all over the world to ride the demanding trail.

Geology: One cannot cross these lands without some curiosity as to how they were formed. In the area around Moab, the Colorado and Green Rivers have exposed 300 million years of geologic history. The process was extremely complex, with oceans covering the land, leaving deposits, and then retreating. Ten million years ago, the earth's crust was pushed up, forming an area called the Colorado Plateau. Waters flowing off the land formed into streams and rivers which quickly (in geologic time) cut through this high plateau, exposing layers thousands of feet below. Harder layers, like White Rim Sandstone, resist longer than softer layers, resulting in the varying stair-step effect that is prominently seen in the canyonlands. Spires and needles are the result of the more resistant layers that form a protective cap as erosion continues underneath.

The formation of arches started with the massive salt beds under the rock layers described above. This unstable base allowed the overlaying rock to shift and buckle, which formed domes. Cracks formed, slicing the domes like bread. Erosion then rounded the slices into fins. When softer spots on the sides of the fins broke away, pockets were created. Water and ice working on the pockets finally wore through the fin, creating a hole or window. Eventually, as the windows enlarged, only a small part of the fin remained, leaving an arch. As arches age, they become thinner and more dramatic. Eventually arches wear thin and collapse. Some arches are formed from the top down and start as potholes.

Petroglyphs and Pictographs: Petroglyphs are Indian motifs that have been scratched, pecked, or otherwise abraded into hard rock surfaces, often in desert varnish, which provides a contrasting background color. Pictographs are paintings or drawings on rock surfaces using mineral pigments and plant dyes. It's a federal crime to damage or deface petroglyphs or pictographs, commonly called rock art or Indian writings. If you see vandalism taking place, report it immediately.

UTAH OHV LAWS AND LICENSING REQUIREMENTS

Utah OHV Laws have changed frequently and could change again. For the latest information go to **www.stateparks.utah.gov/ohv** or call **(800) 648-7433 (OHV-RIDE)**. The laws are very complex and require some advanced planning, especially for nonresidents. Key issues, as of 2005, are generalized below.

1. Utah residents must display a current Utah OHV sticker on front and rear of their ATVs during operation or transport. These are available through the Utah Division of Motor Vehicles. A registration fee is charged in addition to an aged-based fee on the ATV. Also, as of Jan. 1, 2005, residents are assigned a 5-digit (3 letters and 2 numbers) registration number which must be displayed on rear of ATV in minimum 1-inch block letters in contrasting color. You must paint the digits yourself or buy stick-ons.

2. Nonresident ATVs must display a current home-state OHV sticker during operation and transport. Utah recognizes some out-of-state registrations, which are listed on the above Web site. If your state is not listed, you must purchase a nonresident permit. These are available at most Maverik stations in Utah. (There are two Maverik stations in Moab; see appendix for contact information.) A nonresident application is also available online. If 16 or older, make sure you carry your driver's license to prove your out-of-state residency.

3. No one under the age of 8 (resident or not) is allowed to operate an ATV in the state of Utah. (There are some exceptions for sponsored events.) Children under 8 may ride as passengers.

4. Everyone (residents and nonresidents) between the ages of 8 and 16 must complete an approved education class, pass a test and be certified before they can ride in Utah. Classes are available at various places across Utah. Some out-of-state classes are accepted. Nonresidents should call (800) 648-7433 (selection #2) several weeks in advance to learn about classes.

5. A properly fitted and fastened "DOT" approved helmet is mandatory for operators and passengers under 18 years old. Helmets are optional for adults, but highly recommended.

6. Brakes must be sufficient to stop and hold your ATV. You must have an operating headlight and tail light when riding between dusk and dawn. A brightly colored whip flag, at least 8 feet off the ground, must be used at sand dune areas. Muffler and spark arrester are required.

7. Riding on public lands is a privilege, not a right. Always stay on designated routes and protect your riding privilege. Don't ride on

paved roads except to cross briefly at a right angle. Make a complete stop before crossing and yield to oncoming traffic.

Criminal acts. It is a crime to ride your ATV off the trail, crush vegetation or cryptobiotic crust, cause excessive noise, harass wildlife, vandalize property, remove historical artifacts or cause excessive pollution of air, land or water.

The backcountry of Moab is heavily patrolled by BLM rangers (using ATVs and Jeeps) who take the above offenses very seriously. Ignorance of the law will get you no sympathy. Large fines are commonly paid by violators. Serious violations can result in confiscation of ATVs.

SAFETY TIPS

Helmets. As stated previously, helmets are required by law for operators and passengers under the age of 18. But frankly, the law should be the least of your concerns. Moab's rock is very unforgiving. Even a minor incident can cause a serious head injury or even death. Helmets with chin protectors are best.

Body protection. At minimum, wear gloves, long pants, a long-sleeve shirt, heavy leather boots and eye protection (goggles or face guard). If possible, wear a chest protector to avoid being stabbed by a tree branch or other sharp object.

Speed control. Most accidents occur because of excessive speed. Be especially careful around blind curves. Don't follow too close. Leave your lights on all the time.

Fuel limitations. Know how far your ATV will go on a tank of gas. Check your gas level frequently. If you carry extra gas, make sure it is in an approved container.

Riding at night. Avoid it whenever possible. Trails are difficult enough in the daylight. Allow plenty of time for your return trip. Always make sure your lights are working before you head out. You never know when something will delay you.

Stay together. Keep one another in sight to avoid getting split up. Make sure everyone knows the planned route. If you get separated and don't know what to do, wait along the planned route until your party finds you.

Carrying passengers. Unless your ATV is specifically designed for two people, don't carry a passenger. Many ATVs have room for a second person but are not really designed for it. A driver must be able to shift his weight quickly for balance. A second person on the back changes the weight ratio and restricts the driver's movements. This is particularly dangerous on Moab's steep slopes. Many people, out of necessity, ride double, but it's not a good practice.

Young riders. Riders under the age of 16 should be supervised by a responsible adult at all times. Riders should be tall enough to straddle their machines with both feet on footrests with a slight bend at the knees. Most injuries to children are caused by riding machines too large for their small bodies.

Be alert. Make sure you are well rested. It's a crime to ride while under the influence of alcohol or drugs.

Tell someone your plans. Always tell someone where you are going and when you plan to return. Leave a map of your route. Make sure you tell them when you return so they don't go out looking for you.

Travel with another vehicle. Walking out can be grueling and dangerous. In an emergency, a second vehicle could save a life.

Flash floods. Moab is usually dry; however, storms can move in quickly, bringing a chance of flash floods. A dry stream bed can become a raging torrent in minutes. Wait for water to recede before attempting to cross. If water starts to fill a wash or canyon, exit perpendicular to the water flow. If necessary, leave your ATV and climb to safety. Don't try to outrun rising water.

Clay surface roads. Many roads in Moab, like the Blue Hills Road in the northwest area, are composed of a very greasy clay that becomes impassable when wet. **Stay off these roads if rain is imminent**. Even if you manage to get your ATV back to the staging area, your transport vehicle will likely not be able to get back to the main highway. This is a serious situation that people often overlook.

Changing conditions. Moab's backcountry is fragile and under constant assault by forces of nature and man. Rock slides can occur or an entire road can be washed away overnight. A trail may be closed without notice. Be prepared to face unexpected situations.

Cliff edges. Watch children and pets around cliff edges. Handrails are rarely provided. Watch for loose rock and stay away from these areas when it's wet, icy or getting dark. If you climb up something steep, remember it is always harder to come back down.

Lightning. During a storm, stay away from lone trees, cliff edges and high points. The rubber tires of your ATV can act as an insulator between you and the ground, but stay low. Lightning can strike from a distant storm even when it's clear overhead. Seek shelter whenever possible.

Mines, tunnels and caves. Be careful around old mine buildings. Stay out of mines, tunnels and caves. They may look safe, but noxious gases may be present. Don't let children and pets play in these areas.

Altitude sickness. Some people may experience altitude sickness on mountain trails. Symptoms include nausea, dizziness, headaches or weakness. This condition usually improves over time. To minimize symptoms, give yourself time to acclimate, drink plenty of fluids, decrease salt intake, reduce alcohol and caffeine, eat foods high in carbohydrates and try not to exert yourself.

TRIP PREPARATION

Think ahead. You probably can't prepare for every possible thing that can go wrong, but thinking about it ahead of time will improve your chances. Here are a few things to consider:

Vehicle readiness. Inspect and service your ATV regularly. Check belts, tires, battery, spark plug(s), fluids, lights, loose or worn parts. If you don't do your own wrenching, pay a qualified person to do it.

Know your ATV. It goes without saying, you must know how to operate your own ATV. If renting or borrowing equipment, make sure you are well instructed on its operation. If traveling with a group, share idiosyncrasies of each other's machines.

Check for trail closures. Call the BLM or Forest Service to find out if any trails are damaged or closed. Keep in mind, they may not be aware of damage if it occurred recently. (See contact information in appendix.)

Prepare for an overnight stay. It is not unusual to get stuck on a trail overnight. You'll rest easier if you are prepared.

Check the weather forecast. Weather can make or break your day. Read the section on Moab's weather.

CHECKLIST OF EQUIPMENT AND SUPPLIES

It's daunting to list everything you might need on a trip. Where do you put it all? Try to miniaturize as much as possible. Check your ATV specifications for weight limits and distribute weight correctly front and rear. Everything should be securely tied down or in a carry box.

Basics:

    Water (Carry at least one gallon per person per day.)
    High-energy food (I like Cliff Bars, available all over Moab.)
    Warm raincoat
    Small space blanket
    Small shovel

Large trash bags (can be used for trash or rain protection)
Map, compass (See map suggestions in this introduction.)
Basic tool kit (My ATV came with a tiny tool kit.)
Tow strap
Waterproof matches or magnesium fire-starter
Small flashlight (I like the tiny Maglite that doubles as a candle.)
Small first aid kit and water purification tablets
Toilet paper, suncreen, insect repellent, pencil and paper
Knife or multi-purpose tool
Extra ignition key, prescription glasses, medications
Backup drive belt (need proper tools & knowledge to change)

Other things you may want:

Tire repair plug kit or can of tire sealant
CO2 cartridge gun or hand air pump (I carry an electric pump that
    plugs into 12-volt socket.)
Extra clothing, gloves, coat (or snowmobile suit in cold weather)
More complete set of tools (see suggestions below)
Larger first aid kit with instruction book
Small ice chest or insulated bag, larger choice of foods, drinks
Sleeping bag, small tent
Water purification filter
Large plastic tarp, nylon cords
Signal mirror, whistle, flare gun
Small set jumper cables
Extra gas, oil, fluids
Small fire extinguisher
Baling wire, duct tape, nylon zip ties and string
Extra spark plug(s)
Extra headlight bulb
Small assortment of nuts, bolts, clamps and cotter pins
Small axe or hatchet or folding saw
Cell phone (Regular cell phone is not reliable but take it anyway.
    Satellite phone is best if you can afford one.)
Small handheld CB radio or UHF radio
GPS unit with solid mount
Camera
Extra batteries
Winch or small come-along
Portable toilet (lightweight bag type) where required
Firewood (if camping where wood collection is prohibited)

Suggested tools:
- Open end/box wrenches (check ATV for sizes)
- Small socket set (check ATV for sizes)
- Small adjustable wrench
- Combination screwdriver with different tips
- Spark plug wrench
- Needle-nose pliers with wire cutter, Vise-Grips
- Any special tools required for your ATV
- Low pressure tire gauge

YOUR RESPONSIBILITIES AS A BACKCOUNTRY RIDER

It is estimated that Moab has more than a million visitors every year. They come for many different reasons, including hiking, biking, rafting, fishing, hunting, camping, rock hounding, Jeeping, ATV riding, dirt-bike riding and general sightseeing. Most of these visitors spend at least part of their time in the backcountry. The accumulated result of these large numbers is having a negative effect on the countryside. Hiking and biking trails are widening with more shortcuts appearing. Camp spots are increasing in number and getting bigger. More trash is blowing around and vegetation is being trampled. But worst of all is the proliferation of tire tracks across pristine land. It begins with one selfish or ignorant individual who cuts across an open area. The next person uses these tracks as an excuse to claim a road exists. Before long a new road is formed. Eventually the hillsides are covered with a spaghetti-like network of roads to nowhere.

It has been my observation, in the many years I've been coming to Moab, that the majority of backcountry travelers are well-meaning, responsible people who do their best to follow the rules by staying on what they know are legal routes. Frankly, I've never personally witnessed someone deliberately cut across a fragile open area (legal sand dunes don't count). If I did, I'd do my best to report them immediately. I have seen people widen a trail by going around a mud hole or pulling over at a narrow spot to let someone pass. In these cases, I kindly explain why this should not be done. Obviously, there are people doing damage, but I believe it is a small percentage. Unfortunately, it doesn't take many irresponsible people to spoil it for everyone else.

The Bureau of Land Management and Forest Service, responsible for most of the backcountry around Moab, are working hard to educate land users. Too often, however, their efforts are failing. Sometimes their only recourse is to completely close an area, much to the chagrin of the majority of people who are acting responsibly.

With that as a prelude, here is a list of your responsibilities as a backcountry rider:

Stay on existing routes. If you are not sure that a road is legal, it probably isn't. Designated routes are unquestionably well traveled even though route markers may be illegally removed. If you stay on the routes in this book, you will be okay. I worked closely with the BLM during the route selection process.

Leaving the trail causes unnecessary erosion, kills vegetation and spoils the beauty of the land. Scars remain for years. Don't widen the trail by riding around rocks and muddy spots. Don't take shortcuts or cut across switchbacks. When you have to pass another vehicle, wait for a wide spot. Anticipate where you will pull over when you see an oncoming vehicle. Pull over at wide spots to let faster vehicles pass.

Wilderness areas and national parks. Boundaries for these areas are usually well marked. Riding inside these areas is a very serious offense. Two trails of concern in this book include Potash Road #13, which ends at the border of Canyonlands National Park, and Sovereign Trail #9, which skirts the edge of Arches National Park.

Wilderness study areas. No excuses here. You must stay on marked routes at all times. Even if you think a trail marker has been removed, don't take a chance. Stop and turn around. Frankly, I stay out of wilderness study areas to avoid any confusion. Most of these areas are destined for closure to motorized traffic, anyway. There are so many great places in Moab to ride, I don't feel the need to go into wilderness study areas. The trail of most concern here is Steelbender Loop #25. It is completely surrounded by wilderness study areas, indicated on my map.

Sand Flats Recreation Area. This is a highly sensitive, heavily-used area made up of BLM and state lands. It is managed through a unique partnership between Grand County and the BLM. Routes are clearly designated, and you must stay on them at all times. You must camp in designated sites only, use the vault toilets provided and pack out your trash. You cannot collect firewood, so bring your own if you plan to build a fire. Dogs are allowed but must be leashed or tied up at campsites. In the backcountry, a leash is recommended but not required; however, dogs must be under verbal control and must never chase wildlife. The only trail in this book inside SFRA is Fins & Things #24. It is very clearly marked. Due to several extremely steep and dangerous spots on the southern loop, SFRA does not recommend this portion for ATV use. The new recommended starting point for ATVs is at Diving Board Rock just before mile marker 4.

When you check in at the entrance station, you will be given a beautiful, full-color visitor guide as part of your entry fee. It contains complete rules with photos and maps of all trails in the area, including famous Slickrock Bike Trail, Hell's Revenge 4x4 Trail and Porcupine Rim Trail (multi-use).

Stay off single-track trails. Nothing is more upsetting to a dirt biker or mountain biker than to have the trail widened by an ATV.

Private property. Some trails in this book are public roads that cross private property. These roads are usually well marked. As you pass through, you must stay on the road. You are trespassing anywhere else. Respect the rights of property owners. Pass through quietly, don't disturb livestock and leave gates the way you find them unless signs say otherwise.

Cryptobiotic crust. The black, jagged crust you see everywhere in the desert is called cryptobiotic crust. It forms a base for future plant growth and is nature's first step to controlling erosion and reclaiming the land. In its early stages, it is nearly invisible. It is extremely delicate and takes decades to form. Never walk, ride or drive on it.

Ruins and archaeological sites. It is a federal crime to disturb historical and archaeological sites. This includes petroglyphs and pictographs. Please admire them from a distance and take only pictures.

Bringing dogs. Dogs must not disturb wildlife. Although dogs are allowed in the backcountry (except in national parks), it's not the best place for them. Summers are extremely hot, rock surfaces wear on their paws, cliff edges are hidden and cacti abound. Although leashes are usually not mandated, for your dog's safety, it is best to keep them leashed. (For kennel information go to www.moab-utah.com/pets.)

Trash disposal. Carry bags and pack out your trash. Make an extra effort to pick up litter left by others.

Human waste. The disposal of human waste and toilet paper is becoming a big problem in the backcountry where facilities are not provided. Keep a small shovel handy and bury solid waste 6 to 12 inches deep, away from trails, campsites and at least 300 feet from any water source, which includes dry washes. Put toilet paper and hygiene products in a small plastic bag and dispose with trash. (Consider commercial Wag Bags®. See at www.thepett.com.)

Camping. Generally, BLM and Forest Service camping guidelines allow dispersed camping along the trails. These spots are free, but no services are provided. In some places, camping is restricted to designated sites. Here, you'll find metal fire rings, toilets and sometimes picnic tables. Payment is made via self-service fee stations. Larger BLM campgrounds usually have more facilities and are located in the most popular areas. Some are large enough for RVs and motor homes. Fees range between $5 and $10 per night depending on facilities and locations. Rules and regulations are posted nearby. Camping is on a first come, first served basis except group campgrounds, which must be reserved. (For more information on BLM camping, go to www.blm.gov/utah/moab.)

When selecting a dispersed campsite along the trail, you can usually find a place where others have already camped. Often, rock fire rings have already been built. Do everything you can to avoid camping in a new spot. Rules for dispersed camping include a 14-day limit, packing out your trash, staying 100 feet away from water sources and not leaving campfires unattended. Always make sure your fire is dead out. Douse it thoroughly until it is cold to the touch. In addition, follow these low-impact camping techniques:

1. Don't burn cans, bottles, etc. in your campfire.
2. Use only dead and downed wood where collection is allowed.
3. Use a fire pan whenever possible. (This is a metal tray, like a garbage can lid, that holds ashes, which when cooled can be carried away with your trash.)
4. Heat water for cleaning rather than using soap.
5. If possible, use a propane stove for cooking. It's quick, easy and better for the environment.
6. Don't trample vegetation around the campsite. This causes the campsite to gradually enlarge until it becomes one huge bare area. And above all, don't let the kids ride their ATVs around the campsite.

Commercial campgrounds and RV Parks. Moab has many excellent commercial campgrounds and RV parks in and around town.

Make reservations early. (See listing in appendix.)

Potholes. Moab has a unique feature called potholes. Unlike what you see in deteriorating pavement, Moab's potholes are smooth-walled, bowl-shaped depressions in solid rock created by ice and wind. They can be as tiny as a tea cup, hot tub size or giant pits big enough to hold a house. When dry, these potholes appear lifeless. However, after a rain, they fill with water and teem with microscopic life. Never drive through potholes, wash dishes, swim or bathe in them. This pollutes the water and destroys the microscopic life.

COURTESY AND ETHICS

Riding an ATV in Moab's backcountry is an experience you will remember for a lifetime. On many trails, you can ride for hours without seeing another person. The most popular trails, however, will be shared with hikers, bikers and horseback riders, most of whom are looking for quiet and solitude. Obviously, there is an inherent conflict when ATVs cross paths with non-motorized users.

When I'm on the trail, I do my best to mitigate the situation. I recognize that, although my ATV is quieter than most, it still makes noise and is going to irritate some people. I realize my riding kicks up dust and that, if I don't slow down, somebody's going to get upset. Since I hike and bike myself, it's easy to empathize with their situation. It's even more critical when animals are involved. I certainly don't want to run over anyone's dog or spook their horse.

The title "Courtesy and Ethics" suggests that the following actions are voluntary. In theory, that may be. In practice, however, following these suggestions is critical to the long-term survival of motorized recreation. Fair or not, OHV recreation has a tarnished image. We must all do our best to improve that image.

Overtaking hikers. Slow down well in advance to give time for your dust to settle. Swing wide and pass as slowly as possible. If they have a dog or pack animal, give them time to prepare. You may have to stop completely and shut off your engine. Every situation is different. Allow them an opportunity to give you instructions.

Oncoming hikers. On a wide road, move way over and go by as slowly as possible. On a narrower trail, pull over, shut off your engine and wait for them to walk by. Take off your helmet and exchange courtesies whenever possible. If they have a dog or pack animal, pull over sooner and stop until they are well past before starting your engine.

Overtaking horseback riders. This is the trickiest of all situations. You have to get close enough so they hear you, but not so close to spook the horses. Some horses stand quietly, others may bolt at the slightest provocation. You might have to stop, shut off your engine and walk toward the riders to discuss the situation. They may want to dismount or ride way off to the side. If they ignore you and you are sure they know you are behind them, proceed as cautiously as possible.

Oncoming horseback riders. Pull over, as early as possible, shut off your engine and wait for them to pass. Take off your helmet and exchange greetings.

Mountain bikers. With slow-moving bikers, you handle the situation much the same as hikers. However, it gets more complicated when the bikers are riding fast. If you gradually catch up to them, you might want to slow down a bit and not pass at all. If you can't wait, make sure they know you are behind them, then go just fast enough to get by. You don't want to go too fast, but you don't want to dally beside them either. If bikers approach you from behind, just slow down and let them pass. A smile and a wave really help.

Making your ATV quieter. If you have a loud machine, ask your ATV dealer for suggestions to make it quieter. Make sure the muffler is working properly. Whatever you do, don't alter your existing muffler to make it louder.

Wildlife. It's a crime to harass wild animals. Deer are the most frequent critters you'll see, but many other animals abound. Most scurry off before you know they're there, but sometimes you get lucky and they hang around long enough to snap a picture.

Carry extra water for others: This is a personal thing that I like to do. I've been able to help some desperate people over the years. Most often it's bikers who have underestimated their needs.

RIDING ON SLICKROCK

Riding in Moab's hardrock country is somewhat different than the usual "dirt through forest paths" that most people are accustomed to. Even advanced riders, if they haven't ridden on slickrock before, need to go easy at first until they understand how differently their ATVs respond.

Slickrock is a smooth, super-gripping surface that enables ATVs to climb and descend at very steep angles, often well beyond the recommendations of ATV manufacturers. When climbing a dirt hill, tires spin, which requires additional throttle. You may slide sideways and have to compensate by turning back and forth. Four-wheel drive adds significantly to your gripping power in loose soil. Some ATVs (like mine) are designed to sense rear-wheel spin before four-wheel drive kicks in. The concept works great on loose surfaces, but not as well on slickrock.

When you start up a steep slickrock surface, your tires grip immediately. If you apply too much throttle, your ATV may lurch forward too quickly or even flip over backwards in a worst-case scenario. If you don't apply enough throttle, your ATV can stall, leaving you in a precarious position. You have to be aggressive, but not too aggressive. It's a delicate balance that requires practice. This applies to both automatic and clutch ATVs. On-demand four-wheel drive may not kick in because the rear  wheels don't spin. This reduces the additional traction advantage you would normally gain with four-wheel drive.

Going down steep slickrock is also different. You need to be extra careful not to apply too much front brake, which could cause a tail-over-nose flip.

Steep slopes require tremendous weight shifts to compensate for the extreme angle. It takes extra strength to hold on. This is a prime reason why you shouldn't carry a passenger. If your passenger doesn't lean enough, the operator must compensate.

Side hill situations should be avoided whenever possible. It is very easy to roll over sideways on Moab's tippy slickrock.

It is very important that you use a spotter or two when learning how to ride up or down steep slickrock. Even after you learn, it's a good idea to have a spotter close by.

ROUTE-FINDING TIPS

Route-finding in Moab's backcountry can be very challenging. However, if you have the right tools and know what to look for, you can become quite proficient at finding your way around.

Maps. Before you go anywhere, make sure you have a good topographic map. Fortunately, there are several excellent maps available. For years, the bible for Moab has been the *Moab East* and *Moab West* maps by *Latitude 40°*. These maps are packed with helpful information for all types of activities. This company has recently produced a new map called the *Classic Moab Utah Trails Recreation Topo Map*. It doesn't cover quite as much area as the previous two maps, but it works well for key areas. What I like about the new map is that it includes a great deal of specific information on OHV and Jeep Safari routes. *Latitude 40°* is presently updating and expanding their east and west maps, which are due out soon.

In 2004, *National Geographic* published a two-map set called *Moab North* and *Moab South*. These maps, too, are excellent. They highlight many Easter Jeep Safari Trails although fewer side roads are shown. Both *Latitude 40°* and *National Geographic* maps are printed on durable, waterproof plastic.

As good as these maps are, they still don't cover all the trails in this book. That's why I carry *DeLorme's Utah Atlas & Gazetteer.* This oversize booklet covers the entire state and has quite a bit of back road detail. *DeLorme's Atlas* is also handy for plotting your GPS position.

Other Tips. Make sure you are familiar with BLM and Forest Service trail markers but don't depend on them. They are often removed or vandalized. Keep track of your mileage as best you can; don't guess. If you don't have an odometer, use a GPS unit for mileage. Some of Moab trails, like *Poison Spider* and *Fins & Things,* are marked with white painted symbols, although, at certain times of year, they can be faint.

Watch for cairns (small stacks of rocks) that often mark the trail. They may be knocked over, but you can still recognize them if you pay attention. Cairns are often widely spaced so look far ahead to locate the next one. Sometimes colored ribbons are tied to tree limbs or bushes to mark the trail (usually left over from the Easter Jeep Safari). Look for tire marks and oil drippings on steep rock surfaces. Some trails still show bulldozer tracks in the rock, made when the road was built many years ago.

GLOBAL POSITIONING

Consider buying a GPS unit if you haven't done so already. Prices have really come down and they've become quite simple to use. The unit doesn't have to be fancy, just good enough to provide accurate coordinates. When used with *DeLorme's Atlas*, you can easily figure out where you are. More expensive GPS units have built-in maps and allow you to download and upload information into your computer. You would probably like these features, too, but they are not necessary.

I used GPS while working on this book. Frankly, I've found it to be an indispensable tool. I didn't know how well my unit *(Garmin GPS V)* would work outside with the jarring and inclement weather, but it worked flawlessly. I bought a great mount *(RAM-B-149Z-GA2)* that held it firmly in place on my handlebars. I plug the power cord into my 12-volt power socket and I never worry about batteries. At the end of the day, I download my tracklog and waypoints into the computer and print out my entire route. (See appendix for contact information on GPS companies.)

GPS Settings. All the trails in this book show key GPS waypoints in Latitude/Longitude format in hours/minutes.hundredths of minutes. Don't confuse this format with hours/minutes/seconds which looks similar. Make sure your GPS unit displays in the same format or your readings will appear in error. Set your Datum on WGS 84 or NAD83 (not NAD27).

DESERT SURVIVAL

Self-reliance. Most of us live in populated areas and are accustomed to having other people around when things go wrong. In Moab's remote backcountry, you must be self-reliant. Don't count on anyone else's help.

Take plenty of water. I can't stress enough the importance of carrying and drinking plenty of water—at least one gallon per person per day. Running out of water can be a fatal mistake.

Avoid hottest part of day. On long summer days, try to ride in the morning and evening to avoid the hottest part of the day.

First Aid. Always carry a good first-aid kit. Take a first-aid course and learn the basics. Make sure the kit contains first-aid instructions.

What to do if you have mechanical problems or you get lost. Stay with your ATV. There's always a chance that someone will come along if you stay near the road. Your ATV is easier to see than you are. Seek shade. You're more likely to find a rock overhang than a shady tree. Don't sit on the hot ground. Dig down to cooler sand below. Create your own shade with blankets or a tarp. Drink plenty of water; don't wait until you get thirsty. Wear light-colored, loose-fitting clothing that covers as much of your skin as possible. Wear a hat and use sunscreen. Collect firewood before dark. Build a fire before you need it. If you get lost or separated from your group, stay in one place.

If you're familiar with the area and know exactly how far it is to hike out and are absolutely sure you can make it, consider walking out. Cover up with loose clothing, take plenty of water, food, and rain protection to stay dry. As a last resort, travel at night when it's cooler if the terrain is not too treacherous. Make sure you can see where you're walking.

Try to draw attention to yourself using a whistle or signal mirror. Creating a smoky fire is a difficult thing to do in the desert, but this method could be used as a last resort.

If you have a cell phone, try to find a point where you can get a signal and call for help. Often you can reach Moab if you can see the La Sal Mountains. If you have a medical emergency, call 911. Moab has a search and rescue group that has saved many people. For mechanical problems, there are recovery services available but it can be costly. It's a good idea to get to know a few people in town in case you need help. Better yet, don't go out alone.

If you have a CB radio, broadcast on channel 19 or emergency channel 9. Continue intermittently even if no one responds. Make sure you give your location.

Hyperthermia. When your body overheats it's called hyperthermia. Symptoms include dry, flushed skin, inability to sweat, rapid heartbeat, and a rising body temperature. Hyperthermia is often preceded by cramps. They may not go away by drinking water alone. You may need food or salt. If hyperthermia is allowed to progress, you could collapse from heatstroke, which is extremely serious and can be fatal if not treated quickly.

To prevent hyperthermia, stay in the shade, don't overexert yourself, wear loose-fitting clothing, and drink plenty of water. If work is required, conserve your energy as best as possible.

Dehydration. As your body sweats to cool itself, it dehydrates. You may be drinking water but not enough. Eating may make you nauseous. You won't want to eat or drink. As symptoms get worse, your mouth will become dry, you may become dizzy, develop a headache, and become short of breath. At some point, you may not be able to walk or care for yourself.

You must prevent dehydration before it happens. Drink more than just to quench your thirst. If you must conserve water, rest as much as possible, try not to sweat, and don't eat a lot. Digestion requires body fluids. If you have plenty of water, drink it.

Hypothermia. It gets cold in the desert after the sun goes down. If it rains and gets windy, you could find yourself shivering in no time, especially if you've worked up a sweat during the day. Your hands and feet will become stiff. You may not be able to hold a match and start a fire. Prevention is the key. Put on a jacket before you begin to get cold. Stay dry. Change clothes if necessary. If you get too cold, blankets may not be enough to warm you. Build a fire, drink hot liquids, or cuddle up with someone else.

FINAL COMMENTS

I've made every effort to make this book as accurate and as easy to use as possible. If you have ideas for improvements or find any significant errors, please write to me at FunTreks, Inc., P.O. Box 3127, Monument, CO 80132-3127. Or e-mail to *books@funtreks.com*. Whether you're a novice or expert, I hope this book makes your backcountry experience safer, easier, and more fun.

Map Legend

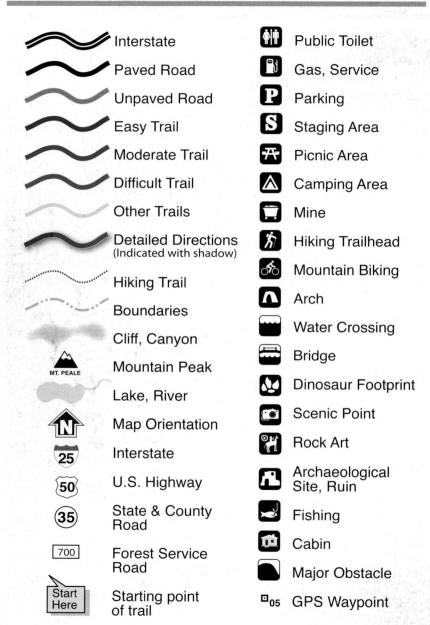

Interstate

Paved Road

Unpaved Road

Easy Trail

Moderate Trail

Difficult Trail

Other Trails

Detailed Directions
(Indicated with shadow)

Hiking Trail

Boundaries

Cliff, Canyon

Mountain Peak
MT. PEALE

Lake, River

Map Orientation

25 Interstate

50 U.S. Highway

35 State & County
Road

700 Forest Service
Road

Start Here Starting point
of trail

Public Toilet

Gas, Service

Parking

Staging Area

Picnic Area

Camping Area

Mine

Hiking Trailhead

Mountain Biking

Arch

Water Crossing

Bridge

Dinosaur Footprint

Scenic Point

Rock Art

Archaeological
Site, Ruin

Fishing

Cabin

Major Obstacle

05 GPS Waypoint

THE TRAILS

Poison Spider Mesa, Trail #12.

Unusual rock formation near Waypoint 03.

Weaving through dry wash.

Watch for colorful wildlife.

Portion of trail climbs to top of ridge.

Desolate terrain in places.

Crystal Geyser is not "Old Faithful."

Crystal Geyser ①

Getting There: From Moab, take Hwy. 191 north about 30 miles to Interstate 70. Go west about 7 miles to Exit 175 (some maps show this exit as 173). Head south on Ruby Ranch Road. After 4.1 miles continue straight under power lines. (Left goes to Tenmile Wash, Trail #3 or back to Hwy. 191 via Blue Hills Road.) You reach the staging area in another 3.5 miles at a major fork.

Staging/Camping: Unload at Wpt. 01 if you are interested in Crystal Geyser exclusively. You can also continue to White Wash Sand Dunes, Trail #2, which offers a larger staging area and primitive camping.

Difficulty: The trail is relatively easy if you stay on the main route described here, but side roads are more difficult. It's easy to get lost if you take a wrong turn. Parts of trail can be impassable when wet.

Highlights: Although not difficult, trail is remote and desolate, providing a true backcountry experience. You may not see another person all day, so be prepared if anything goes wrong. Don't go alone. You'll be disappointed if you take the ride just to see Crystal Geyser. Frankly, it's not much to look at. Don't depend on signs.

Time & Distance: Entire loop, returning to staging area, is 33.5 miles. Allow 3 to 4 hours.

Trail Description: First part of trail follows easy, graded road. After passing a group of oil well tanks, turn right off the main road and drop into a sandy wash. You'll eventually connect to another good road and go past an unusual rock formation (see photo at left). From there, a single-lane road branches north and gradually climbs to a ridge with views of the Green River below. When you reach Crystal Geyser at the river's edge, turn around and return to the unusual rock formation. Bear left and follow a graded road back to where you started.

Other routes nearby: There is a network of fun roads in the Dee Pass Area. (To find the start of these roads, refer to directions in Trail #2.)

Services: Full services in Green River. No services at Exit 175. You may find a gas station open at Crescent Junction, but don't count on it. Gas is also available at intersection of Highways 191 and 313.

Directions: (*Shadowed portion of trail is described here.*)

WP	Mile	Action
01	0.0	*N38° 50.14´ W109° 59.75´* Left (south-west) from staging area.
02	4.1/0.0	*N38° 48.69´ W110° 03.04´* Where major road forks after first oil well tanks, turn right on faint road over small pipe lying on ground. Do **not** follow the main road straight downhill. Path becomes better defined and drops down into dry wash. Bear left in wash.
	4.5	Follow winding wash another 4.5 miles until it runs into larger Salt Wash and turn left.
	4.7	Turn right out of larger wash.
	5.0	Turn left onto good road at unusual rock formation (see photo page).
03	5.4/0.0	*N38° 51.72´ W110° 05.30´* Bear right on lesser road at fork.
	0.9	Turn right at 4-way intersection.
	2.3	Turn left and cross cattle guard.

WP	Mile	Action
	2.9	Follow road to left.
	4.1	Road joins on left. Continue straight.
04	4.7	*N38° 53.83´ W110° 07.16´* Bear right. Road joins on left.
	5.7	Go straight where large road joins on right.
	6.7	View of Green River from high ridge. Stay right as roads go left.
	8.1	Drop downhill into wash and bear right as you join better road. (Remember to turn left here on return trip.)
	8.6	Turn left on major dirt road.
05	9.1/0.0	*N38° 56.29´ W110° 08.10´* Road ends at Crystal Geyser near river. Turn around and retrace route back to Waypoint 03.
03	9.1/0.0	Turn left on good road.
01	5.8	Arrive back at start.

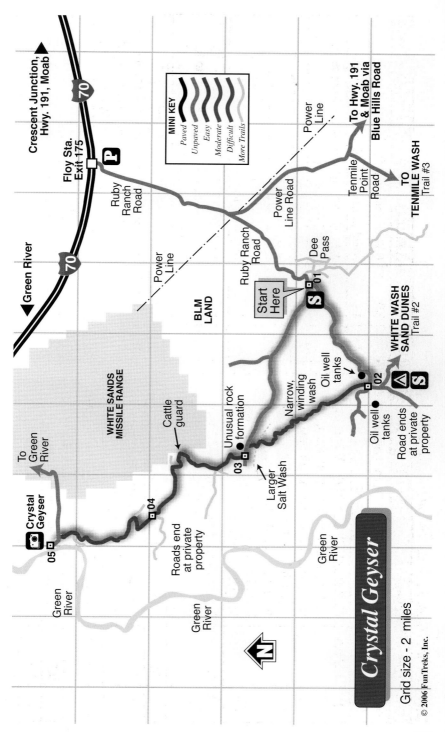

Crystal Geyser

Grid size - 2 miles

© 2006 FunTreks, Inc.

MINI KEY
- Paved
- Unpaved
- Easy
- Moderate
- Difficult
- More Trails

Crescent Junction, Hwy. 191, Moab

▲ Green River

70

Floy Sta. Exit 175

P

Ruby Ranch Road

Power Line

BLM LAND

WHITE SANDS MISSILE RANGE

To Green River

Cattle guard

Unusual rock formation

03

Larger Salt Wash

04

Crystal Geyser

05

Green River

Roads end at private property

Green River

Green River

Narrow, winding wash

Oil well tanks

Oil well tanks

02

Road ends at private property

S

△

WHITE WASH SAND DUNES
Trail #2

Start Here

S

01

Dee Pass

Ruby Ranch Road

Power Line Road

Power Line

Tenmile Point Road

To Hwy. 191 & Moab via Blue Hills Road

TO TENMILE WASH
Trail #3

N

35

Plenty of room to camp at the bottom of the hill near the wash.

Incredible beauty with lots of fun places to ride.

Follow the wash to narrow canyons east of dunes.

Surprises galore.

Explore other trails south of Dee Pass.

White Wash Sand Dunes

Getting There: From Moab, take Highway 191 north about 30 miles to Interstate 70. Go west about 7 miles to Exit 175 (some maps show exit as 173). Head south on Ruby Ranch Road. After 4.1 miles continue straight under power lines. Bear left in another 3.5 miles past the staging area for Trail #1. Go another 4.1 miles past oil well tanks and turn left downhill on a major road. The entrance to the dunes is on the left in another 0.3 miles.

Staging/Camping: You can unload and camp in a large area at the top of the hill or follow the road downhill closer to the wash.

Difficulty: Most of the area is easy to moderate; however, use caution when going over the back side of sand dunes where soft sand can cause a rollover. Some of the toughest places are back in the narrow canyons beyond the dunes.

Highlights: Moab-colored sand and red rock blend together to create this beautiful and popular ATV riding area.

Time & Distance: Allow at least a half day to explore the area. A great place to spend a weekend.

Trail Description: Open riding is currently allowed in the general area of the dunes and along the wide, flat bottom of White Wash. As you head north, then east in the main wash, it narrows and splits into many canyons which eventually dead end. Avoid private property and any other posted areas.

Other routes nearby: Crystal Geyser, Trail #1, is located north of the dunes. The area around Dee Pass (see map) has many unmarked roads that are fun to explore. Heading south from Dee Pass takes you over difficult terrain and eventually connects to the main road that goes to Tenmile Wash, Trail #3. A road departs from the south end of White Wash and connects to other roads in the area. See map for Trail #3 that shows this road and a few key waypoints.

Services: Full services in Green River. No services at Exit 175. You may find a gas station open at Crescent Junction, but don't count on it. Gas is also available at intersection of Highways 191 and 313.

Directions: *(Shadowed portion of trail is described here.)*

WP	Mile	Action
01	0.0	N38° 48.39´ W110° 03.11´ Follow a good road southeast downhill toward White Wash.
	0.3	Road bends left as it goes past parking and camping area. Road gets rougher as it descends. More camping at bottom of hill for high-clearance campers.
02	0.9/0.0	N38° 47.98´ W110° 02.12´ Descend to bottom and enter wash. Continue straight across wash to main part of dunes or turn right to follow wash south. Turn left to follow wash north into canyons.
03	3.2	N38° 47.65´ W110° 00.17´ Canyon splits after heading north in wash. Right side is longer and more interesting. Both canyons dead end. Return the way you came.

WP	Mile	Action
01	0.0	To reach the starting point for trails in the Dee Pass area, head north from Wpt. 01.
	0.3	Turn right, staying on main road.
	4.4	Stay right on the main road past the parking/staging area for Crystal Geyser, Trail #1.
04	4.5	N38° 50.16´ W109° 59.59´ Watch for a small road on the right about 0.1 miles after a cattle guard. The turn is before you cross Salt Wash.
		Note: Once on the trail, head south on the most traveled route. A road soon goes left to Dee Pass. If you continue south, the trail crosses a broad, flat area, then turns left and crosses a fun stretch of rocky, difficult terrain. After approximately 5.3 miles, the trail ends at Tenmile Point Rd.

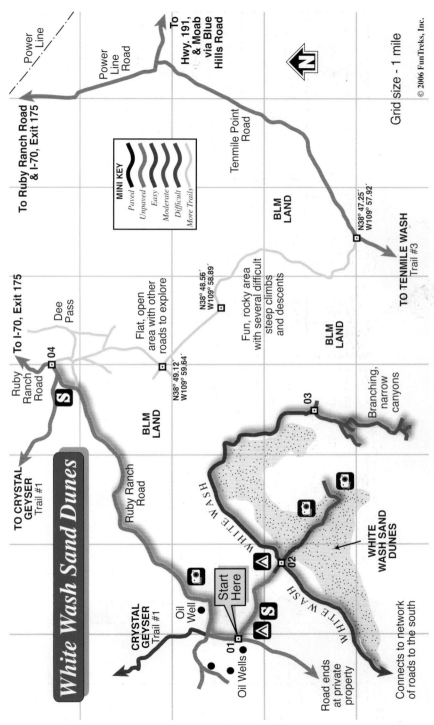

White Wash Sand Dunes

MINI KEY
Paved
Unpaved
Easy
Moderate
Difficult
More Trails

N

Grid size - 1 mile

© 2006 FunTreks, Inc.

To Ruby Ranch Road
& I-70, Exit 175

Power Line

Power Line Road

Power Line Road

To Hwy, 191, & Moab via Blue Hills Road

Tenmile Point Road

BLM LAND

N38° 47.25'
W109° 57.92'

TO TENMILE WASH
Trail #3

Flat, open area with other roads to explore

N38° 48.56'
W109° 58.89'

Fun, rocky area with several steep climbs and descents

BLM LAND

To I-70, Exit 175

Dee Pass

04

Ruby Ranch Road

S

N38° 49.12'
W109° 59.64'

BLM LAND

TO CRYSTAL GEYSER
Trail #1

Ruby Ranch Road

03

Branching, narrow canyons

WHITE WASH

WHITE WASH SAND DUNES

Oil Well

Start Here

A

02

CRYSTAL GEYSER
Trail #1

S

A

WHITE WASH

01

Oil Wells

Connects to network of roads to the south

Road ends at private property

39

Staging area at start of trail can get more crowded than this.

Ski pole measures depth of hole.

Slow down for steep bank.

Repeated water crossings.

Great scenery and a fun place to ride.

Recommend stopping at this boulder choke.

Getting There: From Moab, take Hwy. 191 north about 15 miles and turn left on Blue Hills Road after mile marker 142. At 7.0 miles, continue straight past Dubinky Well Road that joins inconspicuously on left. At 7.2, bear left on Levi Well Road (alternate staging here). After another 6.8 miles, stay right where a road goes south to Spring Canyon Point Road. In another mile you'll reach Dripping Springs, the starting point for Tenmile Wash (downhill through cottonwood trees on left). *Note: Blue Hills Road is impassable when wet.*

From Green River, take I-70 east to exit 175 (some maps show exit as 173). Head south on Ruby Ranch Road 4.1 miles and bear left along power lines. Go another 4 miles and bear right on Tenmile Point Road (not marked). Follow this road about 5.6 miles and turn left toward Dripping Springs. Start of trail is on right in another 1.6 miles.

Staging/Camping: Camping and staging are allowed at the trail head. If coming from Moab, consider staging at start of Levi Well Road and riding your ATV the rest of the way.

Difficulty: Most of the trail is easy, but a few places require climbing and descending steep, sandy stream banks. Heavy rains can change conditions quickly. Flash floods possible.

Highlights: A very popular and environmentally sensitive trail. Stay on marked route at all times. Violations could result in trail closure.

Time & Distance: Allow 3 to 4 hours for 24-mile loop described here.

Trail Description: The main part of the trail winds back and forth across a sandy wash which usually has a small amount of water flowing. It can be much deeper after a rain. The return route climbs out of the wash and loops back over slickrock before connecting to major dirt roads that go back to start. Once out of the canyon, it is easy to get lost because roads are poorly marked.

Other routes nearby: Trails #1, #2 & #4. Trails are connected by a complex network of dirt roads, all open to ATVs.

Services: Full services in Moab and Green River. No services at Exit 175. Gas is available at intersection of Highways 191 and 313.

Directions: *(Shadowed portion of trail is described here.)*

WP	Mile	Action
01	**0.0**	*N38° 44.72´ W109° 57.96´* Head southwest into canyon from staging area.
	0.3	Bear right when you reach a wider canyon. After turning right, the canyon splits briefly. Watch for an invisible deep hole (depth of ski pole) on the right side (see photo). Proceed into the canyon as the marked trail winds back and forth across the stream.
	3.2	Slow down for a steep bank that enters stream (see photo). It could flip you over if you're going too fast.
02	**4.7**	*N38° 43.44´ W110° 00.88´* Bear left at major fork and enter marked dead end canyon. You will return to this point later.
	6.0	Pass through gate. Leave it as you find it.
03	**11.3**	*N38° 41.16´ W110° 03.22´* Cross expanse of slickrock before canyon narrows at boulder choke. **It is recommended that you stop here.** The remainder of canyon becomes muddy, overgrown, very narrow and nearly impassable in spots. Tenmile Wash eventually ends at the Green River. Return to Wpt. 2.
02	**17.9/0.0**	Turn left and climb out of Tenmile Wash. The trail climbs through a large area of slickrock. Follow white dashes painted on the rock.
	0.4	Pass through gate. Leave it as you find it.
	0.7	Bear right.
	1.1	Turn left.
04	**1.4**	*N38° 43.89´ W110° 01.67´* Turn right on Tenmile Point Road.
05	**3.3**	*N38° 44.97´ W110° 00.16´* Continue straight when road joins on left. (This road goes to White Wash Sand Dunes, Trail #2.)
06	**4.5**	*N38° 45.57´ W109° 59.13´* Turn right to Dripping Springs.
01	**6.2**	Arrive back at start.

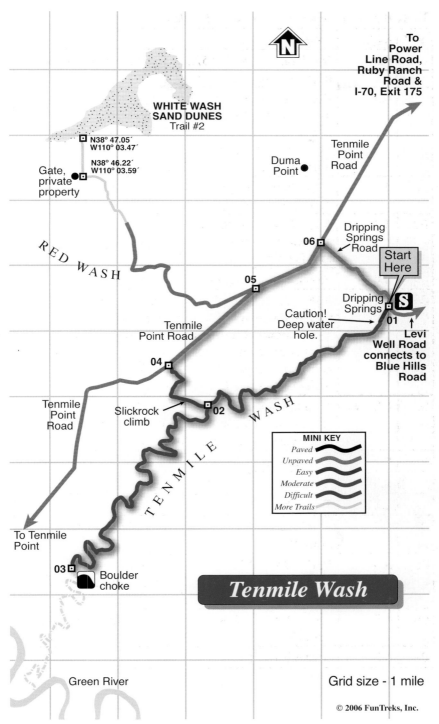

White Wash Sand Dunes
Trail #2

N38° 47.05′
W110° 03.47′

N38° 46.22′
W110° 03.59′

Gate, private property

Duma Point

To Power Line Road, Ruby Ranch Road & I-70, Exit 175

Tenmile Point Road

RED WASH

Dripping Springs Road

06

Start Here

05

Dripping Springs

S

01

Caution! Deep water hole.

Levi Well Road connects to Blue Hills Road

Tenmile Point Road

04

Slickrock climb

02

WASH

TENMILE

Tenmile Point Road

MINI KEY
Paved
Unpaved
Easy
Moderate
Difficult
More Trails

To Tenmile Point

03   Boulder choke

Tenmile Wash

Green River

Grid size - 1 mile

© 2006 FunTreks, Inc.

43

The Needles with Tombstone Rock at right. Use as landmark from many directions.

The trail passes between these two large boulders.

Be careful coming down this steep ledge.

Rainbow effect from layered rock.

Rainbow Terrace 4

Getting There: Drive north from Moab on Hwy. 191 about 9 miles and turn left on Hwy. 313 towards Canyonlands National Park. Go 8.5 miles and turn right on Dubinky Well Road after the third view area. Stay right at 1.4 miles (easy to miss) where Spring Canyon Bottom Road goes straight. Go another 4.9 miles and turn left on Spring Canyon Point Road just before Dubinky Well. Go about 2 miles to the base of The Needles, where you can park on either side of the road.

Staging/Camping: Unload just east of Waypoint 01. Great primitive camping at Big Mesa Campground on Dubinky Well Road 0.2 miles north of Hwy. 313. (You pass the elevated campground as you come in.) You can also stage here and ride your ATV on all major dirt roads.

Difficulty: Most of this trail is easy except for the mile-long stretch across the rocky terrace. There is one steep, rocky ledge that you must come down that will intimidate novice riders. Be careful and use a spotter if necessary. Flash floods possible in the wash.

Highlights: A short trail, but fun when combined with other trails in the area. Memorable views and unusual colors of rock layers. Don't forget your camera. If you have time, as you're coming in, go a few hundred feet north to see Dubinky Well, just before you turn left on Spring Canyon Point Road.

Time & Distance: Loop measures 12.8 miles. Allow 1 to 2 hours.

Trail Description: You'll head north on Dripping Springs Road, a mix of sand and slickrock. After a short stretch along Levi Well Road, you'll turn south on a road that weaves in and out of a wide, dry wash. The excitement starts as you climb to a rocky terrace along the backside of Tombstone Rock.

Other routes nearby: Tenmile Wash, Trail #3, is only a mile to the left when you reach Levi Well Road. Dellenbaugh Tunnel and Secret Spire, Trail #5, are just south and west of Tombstone Rock.

Services: Gas and supplies are available at Archview Campground at the intersection of Highways 191 and 313. Vault toilet at the view area near start of Dubinky Well Road.

Directions: *(Shadowed portion of trail is described here.)*

WP	Mile	Action
01	**0.0**	*N38° 41.18´ W109° 55.17´* Continue west on Spring Canyon Point Road from The Needles.
02	**1.6/0.0**	*N38° 41.49´ W109° 56.61´* Bear right on Dripping Springs Road.
	4.2	Bear left at fork.
	4.4	Turn right on Levi Well Road.
03	**4.8/0.0**	*N38° 44.93´ W109° 56.68´* Turn right off Levi Well Road onto lesser road that heads south.
	0.7	Stay right on road.
	0.8	Road drops into wash, then weaves in and out of wash for several miles.
04	**4.1**	*N38° 42.38´ W109° 54.71´* Turn left at fork.
	4.3	Leave sandy section and begin climb up to rocky terrace.
	4.6	Pass between two giant boulders and follow cairns across terrace.
	4.8	Trail descends steeply off rocky terrace. Study ledge carefully to determine easiest way down. Be careful. Use spotter if necessary.
	5.1	Stay right as you join another road. Follow cairns across open slickrock.
	6.1	Road becomes sandy again.
01	**6.4**	Arrive back at starting point.

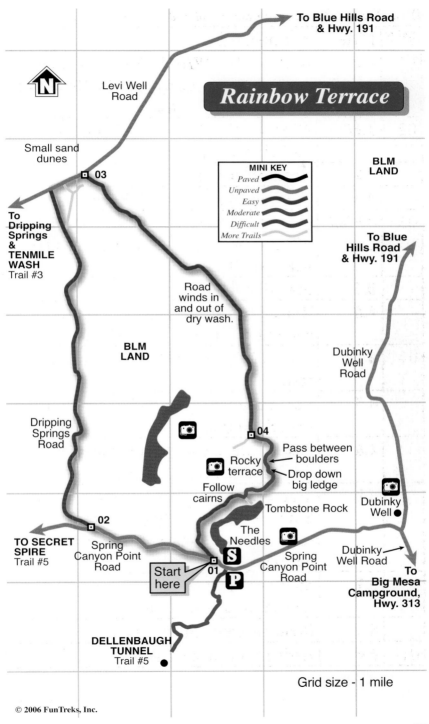

Rainbow Terrace

To Blue Hills Road & Hwy. 191

Levi Well Road

N

Small sand dunes

☐ 03

To Dripping Springs & TENMILE WASH Trail #3

BLM LAND

MINI KEY
Paved
Unpaved
Easy
Moderate
Difficult
More Trails

BLM LAND

To Blue Hills Road & Hwy. 191

Road winds in and out of dry wash.

BLM LAND

Dubinky Well Road

Dripping Springs Road

☐ 04

Pass between boulders

Rocky terrace

Drop down big ledge

Follow cairns

Tombstone Rock

Dubinky Well ●

02

TO SECRET SPIRE Trail #5

Spring Canyon Point Road

The Needles

S

01

P

Spring Canyon Point Road

Dubinky Well Road

To Big Mesa Campground, Hwy. 313

Start here

DELLENBAUGH TUNNEL Trail #5 ●

Grid size - 1 mile

© 2006 FunTreks, Inc.

47

Exiting Dellenbaugh Tunnel.

Secret Spire.

Tombstone Rock beyond Spring Canyon.

Explore area south of Spring Canyon.

8-ft. deep, water-carved red rock trench.

Dellenbaugh Tun., Sec. Spire

Getting There: Drive north from Moab on Hwy. 191 about 9 miles and turn left on Hwy. 313 towards Canyonlands National Park. Go 8.5 miles and turn right on Dubinky Well Road after the third view area. Stay right at 1.4 miles (easy to miss) where Spring Canyon Bottom Road goes straight. Go another 4.9 miles and turn left on Spring Canyon Point Road just before Dubinky Well. Go about 2 miles to the base of The Needles where you can park on either side of the road.

Staging/Camping: Unload at Waypoint 01. Great primitive camping is available at Big Mesa Campground on Dubinky Well Road 0.2 miles north of Hwy. 313. (You pass the elevated campground as you come in.) You can also stage here and ride your ATV on main dirt roads.

Difficulty: Slickrock sections are steep in places but not difficult. If you explore other roads south of Spring Canyon, you'll encounter a few difficult spots (see map).

Highlights: Great riding area includes a fun hike through Dellenbaugh Tunnel with dramatic views of Spring Canyon and Tombstone Rock after you go through the tunnel. Note dangerous cliffs along edge of Spring Canyon. People of all ages enjoy visiting Secret Spire. Search for water-carved red rock trench on way to Dellenbaugh Tunnel.

Time & Distance: As described, about 11 miles. Allow 2-4 hours depending upon how much sightseeing you want to do.

Trail Description: First head south from Tombstone Rock to popular Dellenbaugh Tunnel. Return to start, then head west to see dramatic Secret Spire. After Secret Spire, continue west over interesting slickrock terrain, then return to start via Spring Canyon Point Road.

Other routes nearby: Trails #3 and #4. Many roads to explore south of Spring Canyon and north of Spring Canyon Bottom Road. These roads are not well marked and it is easy to get lost. See map for scattered waypoints at key intersections.

Services: Gas and supplies are available at Archview Campground at the intersection of Highways 191 and 313. Vault toilet at the view area near start of Dubinky Well Road.

Directions: *(Shadowed portion of trail is described here.)*

WP	Mile	Action
01	0.0	*N38° 41.08´ W109° 55.05´* Head south from staging area on single-lane road.
	0.2	Bear left and drop downhill through steep slickrock.
02	0.8	*N38° 40.52´ W109° 55.32´* Enter wide, dry wash at bottom of hill. Turn right and follow main part of wash. It gradually turns south and narrows. (Left in wash takes you to area south of Spring Canyon.)
	1.2	Wash ends at large area of slickrock at northeast end of Spring Canyon. Follow cairns left around end of canyon, then bear right following better defined road. (Note: If you are interested in seeing the water-carved trench shown on photo page, follow drainage to edge of canyon. Caution: dangerous cliffs.
03	1.8	*N38° 41.19´ W109° 55.78´* After a fun, roller-coaster ride over undulating slickrock, you arrive at loop parking area for Dellenbaugh Tunnel. (***Do not ride beyond this point.***) Follow signs and cairns on short hike to

WP	Mile	Action
		tunnel. You must climb down a steep rock wall into a depression to reach tunnel entrance.
01	3.6/0.0	Return to staging area and bear left (west) on Spring Canyon Point Road.
	1.6	Stay left where road goes right to Dripping Springs.
04	2.6	*N38° 41.35´ W109° 57.58´* After cattle guard, turn left on lesser road. Cross short section of slickrock and stay right when road forks again.
05	3.0	*N38° 41.07´ W109° 57.81´* Stay left and stop at end of road. Walk to Secret Spire in view. To continue west after seeing Secret Spire, return to last fork at Waypoint 05 and turn left. Follow trail west over undulating slickrock. Trail is not marked but faint tire tracks help define the route.
06	3.9	*N38° 41.02´ W109° 58.49´* Turn right on Spring Canyon Point Road and follow it east back to start.

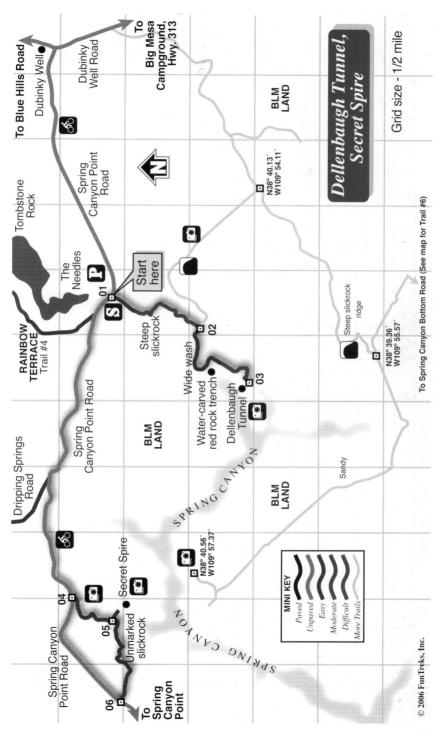

Dellenbaugh Tunnel, Secret Spire

Grid size - 1/2 mile

To Blue Hills Road

Dubinky Well

Dubinky Well Road

To Big Mesa Campground, Hwy. 313

BLM LAND

N38° 40.13′
W109° 54.11′

N

Tombstone Rock

Spring Canyon Point Road

The Needles

P

S 01

Start here

RAINBOW TERRACE Trail #4

Steep slickrock

02

Wide wash

Water-carved red rock trench

Dellenbaugh Tunnel

03

Steep slickrock ridge

N38° 39.36′
W109° 55.57′

To Spring Canyon Bottom Road (See map for Trail #6)

Dripping Springs Road

Spring Canyon Point Road

BLM LAND

SPRING CANYON

BLM LAND

Sandy

N38° 40.56′
W109° 57.37′

Secret Spire

04

05

Unmarked slickrock

SPRING CANYON

Spring Canyon Point Road

06

To Spring Canyon Point

MINI KEY
Paved
Unpaved
Easy
Moderate
Difficult
More Trails

© 2006 FunTreks, Inc.

51

Dramatic shelf road drops into canyon.

Bottom of Spring Canyon.

Trail follows edge of Green River.

Early spring water crossing.

Rocky challenges along the way.

Old truck at Hey Joe Mine.

Hey Joe Canyon ◆6

Getting There: Drive north from Moab on Highway 191 about 9 miles and turn left on Highway 313 towards Canyonlands National Park. Go 8.5 miles and turn right on Dubinky Well Road after the third view area. Bear left at 1.4 miles on Spring Canyon Bottom Road. Continue west 6 more miles to intersection where a good size road goes right. Recommend staging at this point.

Staging/Camping: In addition to the above staging point, you can also unload at a larger staging area 2 more miles down the road; however, Spring Canyon Bottom Road gets rougher as you proceed. Also consider staging at Big Mesa Campground located near the start of Dubinky Well Road. This campground is ideal for large campers and motor homes.

Difficulty: Rocky in places with extremely dense brush. You may find a deep water crossing in early spring when Green River is high. Much of trail is easy to moderate. Along river's edge, trail is very narrow and partially washed out in places. The shelf road that drops into canyon is wide and easy, but sheer cliffs require close attention. Remote location. Don't go alone. Best ridden on a cool, dry day.

Highlights: Awesome views dropping into Spring Canyon and climbing up into Hey Joe Canyon. Interesting mining equipment scattered outside Hey Joe Mine. Use caution around mines. Take insect repellent.

Time & Distance: 31 miles round trip. Allow 3 to 5 hours.

Trail Description: Follow Spring Canyon Bottom Road as it winds downhill into Spring Canyon then traverses along canyon walls to the Green River. Narrow road runs along edge of river far below Spring Canyon Point. Last half mile climbs rocky shelf road into Hey Joe Canyon and ends at Hey Joe Mine. Return over same route.

Other routes nearby: From the starting point, a road goes north and connects to a network of confusing trails south of Spring Canyon.

Services: Gas and supplies are available at Archview Campground at the intersection of Highways 191 and 313. Vault toilet at the view area near start of Dubinky Well Road.

Directions: *(Shadowed portion of trail is described here.)*

WP	Mile	Action
01	0.0	*N38° 37.64´ W109° 55.68´* Continue west on Spring Canyon Bottom Road from staging area.
	2.0	Continue straight past a second staging area on the right. This one is larger but getting there is a bit rougher.
	3.3	Begin descent into Spring Canyon.
	3.5	Shelf road begins. Dangerous cliffs. Go slow and be very careful.
02	4.5	*N38° 38.70´ W109° 59.11´* Cross small creek at bottom of canyon. Follow wide shelf road through canyon toward river.
03	6.2	*N38° 37.53´ W109° 59.79´* Stay right at fork. (Left continues a short distance.)
	6.5	Stay right again and follow road as it curves right and begins to follow the river. Close gate after passing through.
	7.3	Water crossing can be deep at times. See photo page.

WP	Mile	Action
	12.2	Very narrow stretch along river prone to partial washouts.
	13.7	Pass through tunnel of thick tamarisk. More tight brush follows.
	14.9	Bear right uphill into Hey Joe Canyon. When I was there, an old bulldozer marked this location.
	15.2	Difficult rocky spot on narrow shelf road that climbs into canyon.
04	15.5	*N38° 38.46´ W110° 02.27´* Trail dead ends at Hey Joe Mine. Large mine opening can be seen to right. Old mining camp is strewn with discarded mining equipment. Turn around and go back out the way you came.

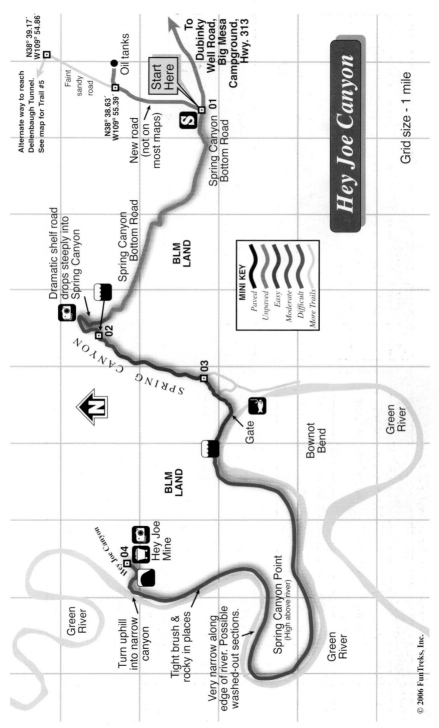

Hey Joe Canyon

Grid size - 1 mile

N38° 39.17'
W109° 54.86'

Alternate way to reach
Dellenbaugh Tunnel.
See map for Trail #5

Oil tanks

Faint
sandy
road

Start
Here

N38° 38.63'
W109° 55.39'

New road
(not on
most maps)

Spring Canyon
Bottom Road

To
Dubinky
Well Road,
Big Mesa
Campground,
Hwy. 313

Dramatic shelf road
drops steeply into
Spring Canyon

Spring Canyon
Bottom Road

BLM
LAND

SPRING CANYON

N

MINI KEY

Paved
Unpaved
Easy
Moderate
Difficult
More Trails

Gate

Bownot
Bend

Green
River

BLM
LAND

Hey Joe Canyon

Hey Joe Mine

Green
River

Turn uphill
into narrow
canyon

Tight brush &
rocky in places

Very narrow along
edge of river. Possible
washed-out sections.

Spring Canyon Point
(High above river)

Green
River

© 2006 FunTreks, Inc.

55

Rocky terrain around Determination Towers.

A few steep climbs.

Pass through this rock opening after towers.

Entering Tusher Tunnel.

Returning from Tusher Tunnel across sandy ridge to rejoin Tusher Wash.

Determination Towers

Getting There: Drive north from Moab on Highway 191 about 13 miles and turn left on Mill Canyon Road just after mile marker 141. Head west over railroad tracks and continue 0.7 miles to a broad intersection where Mill Canyon Road goes left to Cotter Mine Road. Staging is permitted in a wide area to the right of this intersection. (Ignore the first parking area on the right just after the railroad tracks.)

Staging/Camping: Unload at Waypoint 01 as stated above. You can also stage at the other end of Cotter Mine Road and reach the trail from the south side. This entry point is convenient to Archview C.G.

Difficulty: Moderate rock ledges, soft sand and steep climbs. A complex network of roads can be confusing.

Highlights: This route serves as an introduction to a broad, scenic area with many fun roads and dramatic rock formations, including Monitor and Merrimac Buttes and Determination Towers. An exciting side trip to Tusher Tunnel includes twisting sand trails and undulating terrain. Stay on existing roads at all times. No cross-country travel allowed.

Time & Distance: About 15 miles as described here. Allow 3 to 4 hours. Add more time for other roads you'll want to explore.

Trail Description: Climb rocky switchbacks to a high plateau. After a long straightaway across Courthouse Pasture, you'll turn north, then west past the eye-popping Determination Towers. Continue west downhill through twisting, sandy terrain to Tusher Wash. This wide, easy wash goes north toward Tusher Wash Road. Before you reach Tusher Wash Road, turn west to see interesting Tusher Tunnel, which requires a short, steep hike. Return to Tusher Wash where it connects to Tusher Wash Road, then head east back to start.

Other routes nearby: Sevenmile Rim, Trail #8. Numerous other roads shown on map. *Special Note: Trails through Mill Canyon and around Courthouse Rock are important mountain biking routes. Please stay out of this area. These routes may soon be closed to motorized traffic.*

Services: Gas and supplies are available at Archview Campground at the intersection of Highways 191 and 313. No toilets on trail.

Directions: *(Shadowed portion of trail is described here.)*

WP	Mile	Action
01	**0.0**	*N38° 43.53´ W109° 43.95´* Head south on Cotter Mine Road. Stay left on main road past several roads that branch to right.
02	**2.4/0.0**	*N38° 42.01´ W109° 42.60´* Bear right uphill on 7-Mile Road. Switchbacks become rockier at top.
	0.9	Bear right at fork after rocky switchback.
03	**1.1**	*N38° 41.51´ W109° 42.84´* Turn right, leaving 7-Mile Rim Trail.
	1.4	Continue straight on best road at major crossroads. Road bends southwest and heads directly towards Merrimac Butte.
	2.4	Bear right at Y.
04	**3.5**	*N38° 40.16´ W109° 44.57´* Make a hard right at major 5-way intersection and head due north.
05	**4.4**	*N38° 40.96´ W109° 44.62´* Turn left towards Determination Towers.
	4.7	Stay right of towers and pass through right side of rock opening. Descend through sandy, undulating area. Stay right.
	5.9	Stay right as trail drops into narrow wash.
06	**6.2**	*N38° 41.76´ W109° 45.82´* Trail runs into Tusher Wash. Turn right and follow wide wash. It soon passes through a narrow, wet section.
07	**7.3/0.0**	*N38° 42.64´ W109° 45.54´* To reach Tusher Tunnel, turn left uphill out of Tusher Wash on a steep trail. (Don't be confused by 7-Mile sign.) Straight goes directly to Tusher Wash Road in 0.8 miles. Right goes to a fun network of roads, one of which goes to a remote overlook of Mill Canyon.
	1.2	After a series of steep hills (see photo), bear left at fork as you come downhill. Right goes back to Tusher Wash across a sandy ridge.
08	**1.3**	*N38° 42.82´ W109° 46.39´* Continue straight uphill where four roads converge at bottom of sandy wash. (You'll return here later.)
	1.7	Turn left at "T." Right goes northeast to Tusher Wash Road.
09	**2.0**	*N38° 42.66´ W109° 46.96´* Bear left at fork that is part of loop at base of Tusher Tunnel. Find sign and hike up steep path to tunnel entrance. After visiting tunnel, turn around and ride back to Waypoint 08. (Before doing this, you may wish to explore a fun area on the backside of tunnel. Follow road around rocks south of tunnel.)
08	**2.7/0.0**	After returning to Wpt. 08, bear left at bottom of wash and connect to sandy ridge that goes back to Tusher Wash.
10	**0.8/0.0**	*N38° 43.15´ W109° 45.75´* Drop into Tusher Wash and turn left to connect with Tusher Wash Road. Turn right on Tusher Wash Road, which soon crosses a wide part of Tusher Wash.
	0.1	Turn right uphill out of Tusher Wash. Important turn is easy to miss.
01	**2.1**	Arrive back at start.

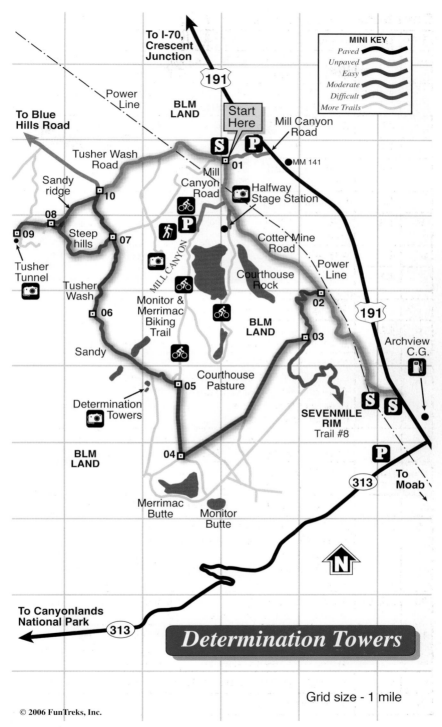

MINI KEY
Paved
Unpaved
Easy
Moderate
Difficult
More Trails

To I-70,
Crescent
Junction

191

To Blue
Hills Road

Power
Line

BLM
LAND

Start
Here

S   P

01

Mill Canyon
Road

MM 141

Tusher Wash
Road

Sandy
ridge

10

Mill
Canyon
Road

Halfway
Stage Station

08

09

07

Steep
hills

P

Tusher
Tunnel

Cotter Mine
Road

MILL CANYON

Power
Line

02

Tusher
Wash

06

Monitor &
Merrimac
Biking
Trail

Courthouse
Rock

191

Sandy

Determination
Towers

05

Courthouse
Pasture

BLM
LAND

03

Archview
C.G.

BLM
LAND

04

SEVENMILE
RIM
Trail #8

S S

P

Merrimac
Butte

Monitor
Butte

313

To
Moab

N

To Canyonlands
National Park

313

Determination Towers

Grid size - 1 mile

© 2006 FunTreks, Inc.

59

The trail itself begins here at Waypoint 02.

Uranium Arch can be viewed from above or below.

Along the rim.

La Sal Mountains and Highway 191 as seen from south side of rim.

Merrimac and Monitor Buttes can be seen from many directions.

Sevenmile Rim

Getting There: Drive north from Moab about 9 miles on Highway 191. Continue past Highway 313 about 0.6 miles to wide gravel road on left.

Staging/Camping: You can unload at a large gravel area next to the highway or drive in a short distance to another staging area next to the railroad tracks. Commercial camping is available just across Highway 191 at Archview Campground. You can also unload at the staging area for Trail #7.

Difficulty: Challenging rock ledges are scattered along the route, but much of the trail is easy to moderate. The side trip to Uranium Arch is a bit steep in places but well worth the effort. The stretch across Courthouse Pasture is fast and easy. Much of the trail crosses open slickrock which makes route-finding confusing at times. Fortunately, the natural flow around the rim helps guide you. Merrimac and Monitor Buttes are handy landmarks that help you find your way.

Highlights: High views along the rim. Looking east you can see the La Sal Mountains and the "Windows" area of Arches National Park. Many fun side roads to explore, but stay on existing roads. No cross-country travel is allowed.

Time & Distance: Complete loop is 15.1 miles. Allow about 3 hours.

Trail Description: Climb rocky switchbacks to a high, slickrock plateau which looks down on Highways 191 and 313. Visit an overlook south of Monitor Butte then continue around the base of Monitor and Merrimac Buttes. Finish with a swift trip across sandy Courthouse Pasture.

Other routes nearby: Combine this route with Determination Towers, Trail #7. An interesting trail with an extreme tippy spot goes around the southwest side of Merrimac Butte. *Note: Trails through Mill Canyon and around Courthouse Rock are important mountain biking routes. Please stay out of this area. These routes may soon be closed to motorized traffic.*

Services: Gas and supplies are available at Archview Campground at the intersection of Highways 191 and 313.

Directions: *(Shadowed portion of trail is described here.)*

WP	Mile	Action
01	**0.0**	*N38° 40.83´ W109° 41.56´* Head northwest on Cotter Mine Road from Highway 191.
	0.4	Cross railroad tracks and swing right.
	1.2	Bear left and climb hill.
02	**2.0./0.0**	*N38° 42.01´ W109° 42.60´* Bear left off Cotter Mine Road at sign for 7-Mile Rim. Follow road west uphill. Switchbacks get rockier near the top.
03	**1.1**	*N38° 41.51´ W109° 42.84´* Bear left at 3-way intersection with bush in middle. You'll return here later.
	1.9	Bear left downhill at big ledge. Look for easiest spot.
	2.8	Start of scenic rim. Continue south.
04	**3.5/0.0**	*N38° 40.56´ W109° 42.28´* Turn right for side trip to Uranium Arch. (White paint on rock says "ARCH.") Return to this point and continue along rim.
	0.8	Turn right at "T" and begin heading downhill. Left goes to overlook. It's hard to see the trail here. Just keep following the general contour of the rim. A road begins to form as you come down off the slickrock.
	2.1	Continue straight at 4-way intersection.
	2.3	Bear right. Minor overlook to left.
05	**2.6**	*N38° 39.50´ W109° 43.48´* Left to major overlook.
06	**3.4**	*N38° 39.01´ W109° 43.73´* Turn around at overlook.
05	**4.2/0.0**	Bear left and continue north.
	0.4	Turn left.
	0.8	After several intersections, bear left again.
	1.2	Turn right before tall ledge that climbs to higher level of slickrock. Follow slickrock around base of Merrimac Butte curving to the left.
07	**1.9**	*N38° 40.16´ W109° 44.57´* Hard right at major 5-way intersection. Sign says "Spur to Buttes."
	2.9	Stay left. Road joins on right.
03	**4.3**	Road curves to right and rejoins Sevenmile Rim at 3-way intersection. Bear left downhill.
01	**5.4**	Retrace route back to start at Highway 191.

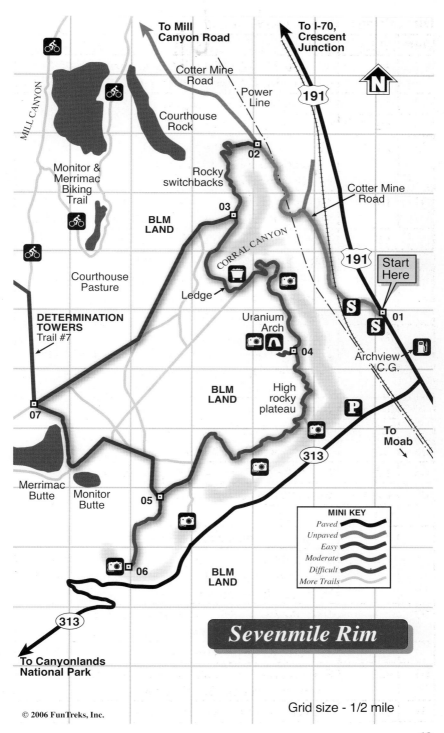

To Mill
Canyon Road

To I-70,
Crescent
Junction

Cotter Mine
Road

Power
Line

N

191

Courthouse
Rock

02

MILL CANYON

Rocky
switchbacks

Cotter Mine
Road

03

191

Monitor &
Merrimac
Biking
Trail

BLM
LAND

CORRAL CANYON

Start
Here

S

S

01

Courthouse
Pasture

Ledge

Uranium
Arch

Archview
C.G.

**DETERMINATION
TOWERS**
Trail #7

04

07

BLM
LAND

High
rocky
plateau

P

To
Moab

313

Merrimac
Butte

Monitor
Butte

05

313

06

BLM
LAND

MINI KEY

Paved
Unpaved
Easy
Moderate
Difficult
More Trails

313

**To Canyonlands
National Park**

© 2006 FunTreks, Inc.

Sevenmile Rim

Grid size - 1/2 mile

63

Staging area just off Highway 191.

Follow signs for ATV Loop.

Obey the rules!

Pipeline Road is steep and rough in places.

Difficult hill on southern loop.

Route-finding can be challenging across open slickrock.

Sovereign Trail

9

Getting There: Drive north from Moab on Highway 191. Turn right on Dalton Well Road 0.6 miles north of mile marker 139 about 3 miles after Highway 313.

Staging/Camping: Unload near large trees east of the highway. Dispersed camping allowed up to 15 days. Archview Campground, located across from Highway 313, is a full-service RV park.

Difficulty: The central loop, described here, is a mix of easy and moderate trails. Small rock ledges and mildly steep hills are scattered along the trail. Route-finding is challenging at times. The northern and southern loops (not described in detail) are more difficult. The southern loop has a very steep hill that is difficult in both directions. Only advanced riders should attempt this hill.

Highlights: Narrow, winding trails over sand and slickrock. Most routes are clearly marked. Single-track trails are for dirt bikes and mountain bikes only. For information and a complete, detailed map of the Sovereign Trail System, contact www.ridewithrespect.org.

Time & Distance: The loop described here is 13 miles and takes at least one to two hours. You can easily spend a full day exploring the other two loops and other roads in the area.

Trail Description: After heading northeast, you'll turn south, winding back and forth over interesting slickrock and sandy valleys. After a short turn east on Willow Springs Road, you'll turn north along a rough, sometimes steep, pipeline service road. From there, you'll head northwest and drop into a narrow valley, followed by a long stretch of interesting slickrock. Finally, you'll turn southwest and return to the start. The southern loop connects to Archview Campground. The difficult northern loop crosses a wide expanse of open slickrock near the border of Arches National Park. Stay out of the national park.

Other routes nearby: Sevenmile Rim, Trail #8, is just across Highway 191 from Archview Campground. Determination Towers, Trail #7, is just two miles farther north on Highway 191.

Services: Gas and supplies are available at Archview Campground.

Directions: *(Shadowed portion of trail is described here.)*

WP	Mile	Action
01	**0.0**	*N38° 42.73´ W109° 42.03´* Head northeast from staging area on Dalton Well Road.
02	**1.5./0.0**	*N38° 43.59´ W109° 40.78´* Bear right off Dalton Well Road at major fork.
	0.3	Bear right on sandy ATV trail. Look for sign.
	2.4	Stay right.
03	**3.9**	*N38° 41.84´ W109° 40.10´* After passing through barbed wire gate, you reach Willow Springs Road. Turn left to stay on central loop.
	4.1	Trail on right at small greenish building marks eastern half of southern loop. Note steep hill (see photo).
04	**4.2**	*N38° 41.91´ W109° 39.78´* Turn left off Willow Springs Road onto marked ATV loop.
	4.8	Stay right where single-track trail goes left in wash. Do not go on single track unless you are riding a dirt bike or mountain bike.
05	**6.5**	*N38° 43.53´ W109° 38.50´* After steep hills, turn left off Pipeline Road. This is a very important turn that is easy to miss. Look for sign.
	7.1	Turn right at "T."
06	**7.6**	*N38° 44.12´ W109° 38.91´* Climb over rocky ridge, then continue straight where road joins on left. Follow undefined trail east over slickrock. Stay to left around base of rocky hillside.
07	**8.6**	*N38° 44.23´ W109° 39.76´* Bear left at "T" and climb out of shallow valley.
	8.7	Stay right where single-track trail joins on left.
	9.7	Continue straight. Left is trail you've already done.
02	**10.0**	Bear left on Dalton Well Road.
01	**11.5**	Return to start.

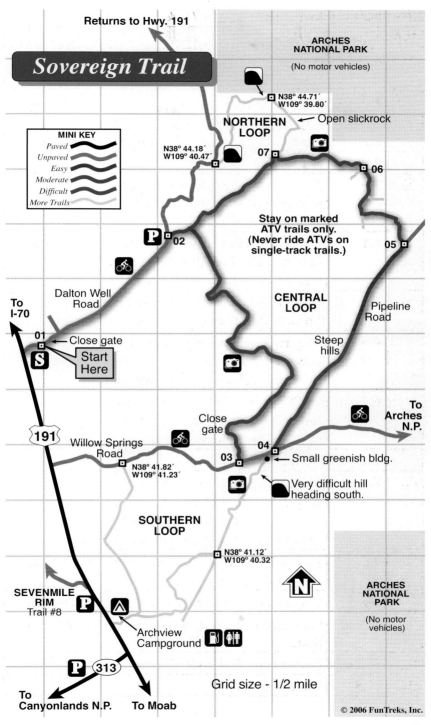

Returns to Hwy. 191

Sovereign Trail

ARCHES NATIONAL PARK
(No motor vehicles)

N38° 44.71′
W109° 39.80′

NORTHERN LOOP

← Open slickrock

MINI KEY
Paved
Unpaved
Easy
Moderate
Difficult
More Trails

N38° 44.18′
W109° 40.47′

07

06

P 02

Stay on marked
ATV trails only.
(Never ride ATVs on
single-track trails.)

05

Dalton Well
Road

CENTRAL LOOP

Pipeline
Road

To
I-70

Steep
hills

01 ← Close gate
S   Start
Here

Close
gate

To
Arches
N.P.

191   Willow Springs
Road

04

03 ← Small greenish bldg.

N38° 41.82′
W109° 41.23′

Very difficult hill
heading south.

SOUTHERN LOOP

N38° 41.12′
W109° 40.32′

N

ARCHES NATIONAL PARK

(No motor
vehicles)

SEVENMILE RIM
Trail #8

P

Archview
Campground

P 313

To
Canyonlands N.P.   To Moab

Grid size - 1/2 mile

© 2006 FunTreks, Inc.

67

Spectacular scenery on shelf road portion of Gemini Bridges Road. Be careful.

Main parking lot is on private land. Fee area.

Distinctive Gooney Bird Rock.

Gemini Bridges.

Four-Arches Canyon.

Extremely difficult Gold Bar Rim.

Gemini Bridges (10)

Getting There: From Moab, take Highway 191 north about 7.5 miles and turn left into large parking area. If you reach Highway 313, you've gone too far. You can also reach Gemini Bridges from the west side off Highway 313. Look for well-marked road.

Staging/Camping: Major parking area at start is on private land and a fee is now charged. Camp along trail in designated BLM sites only.

Difficulty: Road surface is well maintained and very easy. Shelf portion of Gemini Bridges Road is heavily traveled at times.

Highlights: Beautiful scenery on way to remarkable Gemini Bridges—two giant arches at the end of Bull Canyon. The arches are not apparent until you get close and look down. An extremely popular mountain bike route. Please slow down to minimize dust when passing. To view arches from below, see Bull Canyon, Trail #11.

Time & Distance: It is just 8.0 miles to the bridges. Entire trip, described here, is 24.4 miles. Allow 3 to 4 hours for everything.

Trail Description: Enter via a high shelf road with spectacular views. Follow good road through canyon to major "T" where Gold Bar Rim Jeep Trail goes left. You go right uphill. Road levels out with several forks before Gemini Bridges. Park above bridges and hike down the last 0.2 miles. Riding all the way to the bridges is discouraged and could be non-designated by the time you read this. Be extremely careful around the bridges. Watch the kids; there are no handrails. If you wish, continue west after Gemini Bridges to explore Four-Arches Canyon. From there you can return the way you came, or follow the loop described. You can also ride west to Highway 313, then return.

Other routes nearby: Bull Canyon, Trail #11. You can also ride the first part of Gold Bar Rim Jeep Trail before it starts getting too difficult. Advanced riders have ridden the entire trail, but even they need assistance getting down giant 6-feet-high ledges. Metal Masher Jeep Trail is also located in the area (see map).

Services: Gas, supplies and restrooms available at Archview Campground off Highway 191 just north of Highway 313.

Directions: *(Shadowed portion of trail is described here.)*

WP	Mile	Action
01	**0.0**	*N38° 39.37´ W109° 40.63´* Cross railroad tracks at staging area and turn left. Follow road south and climb high shelf road. Drop into valley and head west passing camping area and Gooney Bird Rock.
02	**4.9**	*N38° 36.00´ W109° 40.42´* Turn right at major "T" and climb short hill. Wide road levels out.
	5.4	Bear right where good road goes left to Bull Canyon, Trail #11.
03	**6.5**	*N38° 35.78´ W109° 41.63´* Bear left where good road goes right towards Metal Masher Jeep Trail.
	7.5	Bear left at fork. Right bypasses Gemini Bridges.
	7.7	Stay left at clearing.
04	**7.8/0.0**	*N38° 35.22´ W109° 42.62´* Park your ATV. Hike 0.2 miles left downhill to arches (Gemini Bridges). After visiting arches, return to parking area and head north to reconnect to Gemini Bridges Road, then turn left.
05	**0.9**	*N38° 35.52´ W109° 43.47´* Turn left at "T" to explore Four-Arches Canyon. Drop downhill and pass through gate.
	1.5	Stay right on main road.
	2.0	Stay right again where road goes left to private property. Road narrows and winds downhill into narrowing canyon.
	3.0	Road deteriorates. Right dead ends. Left continues.
06	**3.7**	*N38° 34.13´ W109° 45.25´* Trail ends. Hike beyond this point. Return to Gemini Bridges Road.
05	**6.5/0.0**	Continue west on Gemini Bridges Road.
07	**0.7**	*N38° 35.75´ W109° 44.18´* Turn right at major intersection. Left goes to Highway 313 in about 4 miles.
08	**2.8**	*N38° 36.20´ W109° 42.06´* Right at "T." Left goes to Metal Masher Jeep Trail.
03	**3.6**	Return to Waypoint 03 and turn left.
01	**10.1**	Return to start.

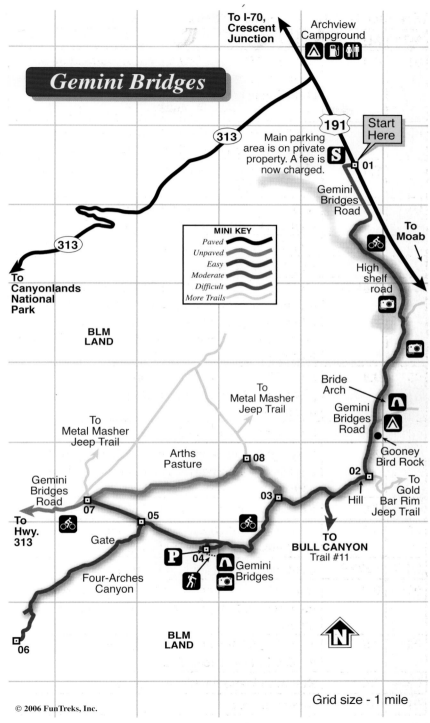

Gemini Bridges

To I-70,
Crescent
Junction

Archview
Campground

191

Start
Here

S
01

Main parking
area is on private
property. A fee is
now charged.

313

Gemini
Bridges
Road

To
Moab

313

High
shelf
road

To
Canyonlands
National
Park

MINI KEY
Paved
Unpaved
Easy
Moderate
Difficult
More Trails

BLM
LAND

Bride
Arch

Gemini
Bridges
Road

To
Metal Masher
Jeep Trail

Gooney
Bird Rock

To
Metal Masher
Jeep Trail

Arths
Pasture

08

03

02

To
Gold
Bar Rim
Jeep Trail

Gemini
Bridges
Road

07

05

Hill

To
Hwy.
313

Gate

P

04

TO
BULL CANYON
Trail #11

Four-Arches
Canyon

06

Gemini
Bridges

BLM
LAND

N

© 2006 FunTreks, Inc.

Grid size - 1 mile

Narrow, winding trails are fun to ride. Stay on existing routes at all times.

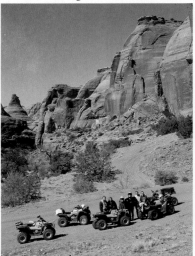

Park here at Wpt. 05 and hike to arches.

Bull Canyon ends at Gemini Bridges.

First side canyon is very scenic.

Day Canyon at Wpt. 07.

Bull Canyon ⑪

Getting There: From Moab, take Hwy. 191 north about 7.5 miles and turn left into large parking area. Unload here. Cross railroad tracks and bear left. Follow Gemini Bridges Road south across high shelf then through canyon. You'll reach a major "T" intersection about 5 miles from parking area. Right at "T" goes to Bull Canyon. (Note: This part of route is shown on map for Trail #10.)

Staging/Camping: Plenty of room to park and unload at the parking area along Hwy. 191. Lot is on private property and a fee is now charged. Camp in designated sites only. Commercial camping available at Archview Campground off Hwy. 191 just north of Hwy. 313.

Difficulty: An easy mix of narrow, rocky wash bottoms and sandy hills. As you approach the ends of side canyons, the routes become more difficult. The first side canyon described splits and ends on narrow shelf roads where it is very difficult to turn around.

Highlights: A fun place to ride with many undulations and narrow, twisting turns. Explore several interesting side canyons. Tremendous view from the bottom of Gemini Bridges. Important: Park at turnaround area (Waypoint 05) and hike short distance to arches.

Time & Distance: From Hwy. 191 to bottom of Gemini Bridges is 9.2 miles. It takes about an hour one way. It's easy to spend a half day or more exploring side canyons and other nearby trails.

Trail Description: You'll enjoy a high, scenic shelf road described in Trail #10 on way to start of this trail. From there, you'll head south to entrance of Bull Canyon. The entrance is narrow and rocky, but soon the canyon widens as the road meanders below towering cliffs. It narrows again before arriving at turnaround area before arches. Interesting side canyons and great views looking down into Day Canyon.

Other routes nearby: Trail #10. You can also ride the first part of Gold Bar Rim Jeep Trail before it starts getting too difficult. See map for another interesting, but very difficult trail through Little Canyon.

Services: Gas, supplies and restrooms available at Archview Campground off Highway 191 just north of Highway 313.

Directions: *(Shadowed portion of trail is described here.)*

WP	Mile	Action
01	**0.0**	*N38° 36.00′ W109° 40.42′* Turn right at major "T" and climb short hill.
02	**0.5**	*N38° 35.81′ W109° 40.87′* Bear left at major fork.
03	**2.1/0.0**	*N38° 34.68′ W109° 40.66′* Make hard right downhill at start of Bull Canyon. Follow narrow, winding wash into widening canyon.
04	**1.7**	*N38° 34.92′ W109° 41.99′* Bear right for Gemini Bridges. Canyon narrows again with a few small challenges. Left here is first side canyon.
05	**2.2**	*N38° 35.08′ W109° 42.31′* Park at sandy loop and hike to arches just around the corner. Do not ride any farther. When finished, turn around and return to Waypoint 04.
04	**2.7/0.0**	Make hard right to reach side canyon (optional). Trail splits after 1.1 miles. Right goes uphill 0.7 miles along narrow ledge road with good views. Left goes downhill and ends in another mile on a very narrow shelf. Turn around before end. Return to start of Bull Canyon.

WP	Mile	Action
03	**7.3/0.0**	At start of Bull Canyon, turn right downhill.
06	**0.1**	*N38° 34.60′ W109° 40.61′* Bear left.
07	**0.4**	*N38° 34.62′ W109° 40.37′* Trail ends at area of small sand dunes that look down into gaping Day Canyon. Return to Wpt. 06.
06	**0.7/0.0**	Turn left to explore another side canyon. This one has no special features, but it's fun to ride.
	2.3	Road fades away as you approach end of canyon. Turn around and return to Waypoint 06.
06	**4.6/0.0**	Left uphill to return to start.
03	**0.1**	Go straight uphill past entrance to Bull Canyon. (If you are interested in the difficult side trip through Little Canyon, watch for a road on the right about 0.3 miles north of Waypoint 03. See map.)
02	**1.7**	Bear right.
01	**2.2**	Back to start. Bear left to return to staging area in about 5 miles. Straight goes to Gold Bar Rim.

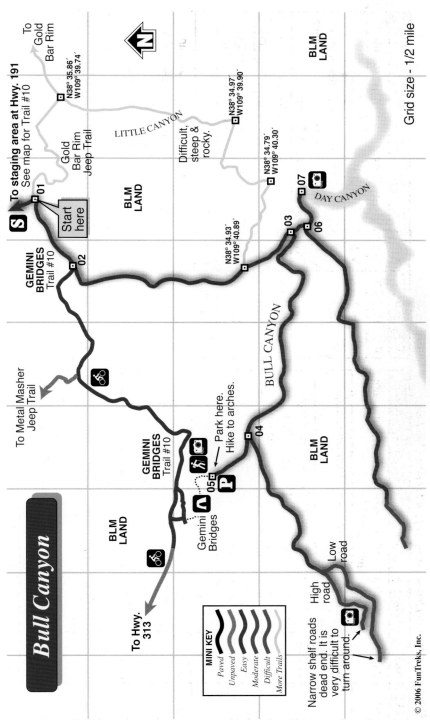

Bull Canyon

To staging area at Hwy. 191
See map for Trail #10

To Gold Bar Rim

N38° 35.86'
W109° 39.74'

Gold Bar Rim Jeep Trail

LITTLE CANYON

Difficult, steep & rocky.

N38° 34.97'
W109° 39.90'

N38° 34.79'
W109° 40.30'

DAY CANYON

BLM LAND

S

Start here

GEMINI BRIDGES Trail #10

N38° 34.93'
W109° 40.89'

BLM LAND

BULL CANYON

To Metal Masher Jeep Trail

Park here. Hike to arches.

GEMINI BRIDGES Trail #10

BLM LAND

Gemini Bridges

BLM LAND

To Hwy. 313

Narrow shelf roads dead end. It is very difficult to turn around.

High road

Low road

N

Grid size - 1/2 mile

MINI KEY
Paved
Unpaved
Easy
Moderate
Difficult
More Trails

© 2006 FunTreks, Inc.

75

Follow this symbol.

Starting up first part of "The Waterfall."

Arch at Waypoint 06.

Faint tire marks help define trail.

Slow down for bikers. Ask if they need water.

Riding skills very important.

Circle around giant pothole.

View of Moab from overlook.

Poison Spider Mesa

Getting There: Drive north from Moab on Highway 191. About 1.5 miles after crossing the Colorado River, turn left on Potash Road 279. Drive 5.8 miles south and turn right into well-marked parking area.

Staging/Camping: Unload at the main parking area. Camping is available off Highway 279 at Williams Bottom Campground on the right just before the parking area. A small fee is charged.

Difficulty: Very difficult and dangerous. Many high rock ledges and tippy spots. For advanced riders only.

Highlights: An unforgettable ATV riding experience for those skilled enough to do it. A very popular Jeep, motorcycle and mountain bike trail that can get busy at peak times. Share the road and be courteous to everyone. Trail is marked with white Jeep symbols (see photo), but it is still easy to get lost. Stay on marked trails at all times. Don't miss arch at Waypoint 06. Follow signs to dinosaur tracks near parking lot. Take plenty of water and a good camera.

Time & Distance: Entire trip, returning to start, is about 15 miles. Allow at least 4 hours. Add for side trips.

Trail Description: Trail begins with rocky climb up steep switchbacks to a broad and beautiful mesa. If you have problems with the switchbacks, don't go any further—it gets much worse. A quarter-mile section beginning with "The Waterfall" will test your riding skills. A few easy sections provide some relief as you proceed. Don't miss a critical turn at Waypoint 02. A white arrow points right to the loop portion of Poison Spider. If you miss this turn, you'll end up on Golden Spike Jeep Trail. This description takes you clockwise around the loop. Jeeps usually go the other way. The eastern side of loop is very confusing. I find it easier to follow this portion of trail from north to south. Two side roads, shown on map, go to incredible overlooks.

Other routes nearby: If you continue on Highway 279 past Poison Spider, you'll end up on easy Trail #13 after the potash plant.

Services: Gas up in Moab. Modern vault toilet located in parking lot at start of trail.

Directions: (*Shadowed portion of trail is described here.*)

WP	Mile	Action
01	**0.0**	*N38° 31.97′ W109° 36.54′* Proceed southwest from parking lot. Trail turns west and begins climb up rocky switchbacks.
	2.4	After an easy stretch, enter a narrow canyon and approach "The Waterfall" (see photo). Follow trail right after second ledge. Two very difficult spots follow.
	2.9	Stay left up steep rock mound to bypass the "V" Notch, a popular Jeep obstacle.
	3.6	Follow trail marker to left where road goes right.
	4.1	Begin easy stretch across flat mesa.
	5.2	Easy stretch ends. Drop downhill and follow switchback to left then sharp right at bottom of hill.
	5.4	Bear left and climb ledge onto slab of slickrock. Look for black tire marks on rock.
02	**5.5**	*N38° 33.72′ W109° 35.78′* Look for white arrow painted on rock that points right. If you miss this important turn, you'll end up on Golden Spike Jeep Trail. Follow arrow off ledge to right.
03	**5.7/0.0**	*N38° 33.76′ W109° 35.63′* Bear left to start loop. Easy to miss this turn. Jeep symbols go both ways.
	0.6	Pass through area of small, fun sand dunes. Continue northwest, then trail turns northeast.
04	**1.7/0.0**	*N38° 34.70′ W109° 35.96′* Bear right to continue loop. Left goes to overlook and Portal Bike Trail.
05	**0.6/0.0**	*N38° 34.43′ W109° 35.66′* Stay right to continue loop. Left climbs steep hill to outstanding overlook with great views and wind-protected alcove.
	0.7	Circle around giant pothole (see photo).
06	**1.1**	*N38° 33.86′ W109° 35.25′* Look for word "ARCH" and arrow painted on rock. Arch should be visible to southwest. Hard right takes you down a dangerous, tippy slope. Better to continue straight then turn right through patch of trees. Follow trail markers back to Waypoint 03 and turn left.
01	**7.3**	Return to start.

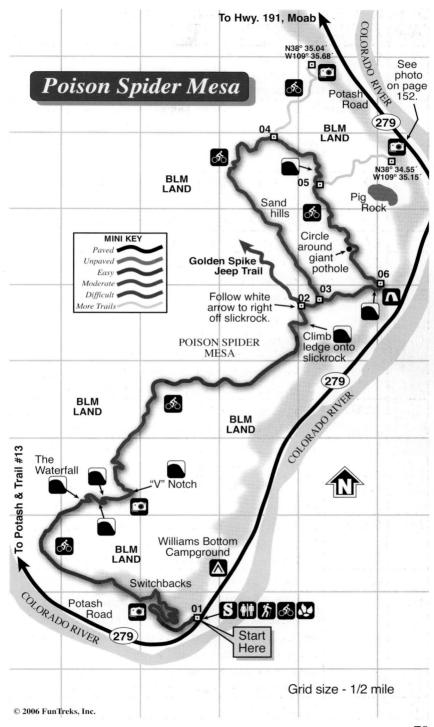

Poison Spider Mesa

To Hwy. 191, Moab

COLORADO RIVER

N38° 35.04′
W109° 35.68′

Potash Road

See photo on page 152.

279

BLM LAND

04

BLM LAND

05

N38° 34.55′
W109° 35.15′

Sand hills

Pig Rock

Circle around giant pothole

MINI KEY
Paved
Unpaved
Easy
Moderate
Difficult
More Trails

Golden Spike Jeep Trail

Follow white arrow to right off slickrock.

06

02   03

POISON SPIDER MESA

Climb ledge onto slickrock

279

BLM LAND

BLM LAND

To Potash & Trail #13

The Waterfall

"V" Notch

N

BLM LAND

Williams Bottom Campground

Switchbacks

Potash Road

01

Start Here

S

COLORADO RIVER

279

Grid size - 1/2 mile

© 2006 FunTreks, Inc.

Staging area next to Colorado River.

Salt company evaporation ponds.

Flowering cacti on desert floor.

Interesting rock formations along the way.

Looking down from Thelma & Louise Point.

Be careful along cliff.

Colorado River as it nears Canyonlands National Park.

Potash Road ⑬

Getting There: Drive north from Moab on Highway 191. About 1.5 miles after crossing the Colorado River, turn left on Potash Road 279. Drive south 16.7 miles along the Colorado River. Pavement ends after going by potash plant. Turn left into parking area next to the river.

Staging/Camping: Unload at parking lot. Camping is not allowed along trail, but you can camp at developed Gold Bar Campground that you'll pass as you drive along Highway 279.

Difficulty: Very easy. A wide, maintained road. Side roads shown on map are also easy, but not maintained. Watch for fast-moving salt mine trucks that cross the road at stop sign at 2.2 miles.

Highlights: Outstanding overlooks high above the Colorado River just outside Canyonlands National Park. Drive along edge of salt company's bright blue evaporation ponds (blue dye accelerates evaporation) in the shadow of towering Dead Horse Point State Park. Stand at point where Thelma & Louise jumped their car into the Colorado River.

Time & Distance: 11.6 miles to national park boundary. Allow 3 to 4 hours for round trip plus extra time for side trips and picture-taking.

Trail Description: Before reaching the trail, you'll follow the Colorado River on Highway 279, a recognized scenic byway. You'll pass the Gold Bar Recreation Site with two campgrounds and parking areas for hiking trails to Corona and Bowtie Arches. Watch for signs for Jug Handle Arch which can be seen on the right. Once on the trail, you'll cross a wide-open plateau located high above the Colorado River but far below Dead Horse Point State Park. Along the way, you'll see dominating Chimney Rock and, if you look real close high above you, notorious Dead Horse Point. (Look for the roof of a pavilion while in the area of Thelma & Louise Point.)

Other routes nearby: Side trips to Pyramid Butte and to overlook beyond Thelma & Louise Point. You drive past the parking lot for difficult Poison Spider Mesa, Trail #12, on the way to this trail.

Services: Gas up in Moab. Vault toilets near boat ramp at start and at Gold Bar Campgrounds along Highway 279.

Directions: (*Shadowed portion of trail is described here.*)

WP	Mile	Action
01	0.0	*N38° 30.41′ W109° 39.64′* Head south from parking lot.
	2.1	Stay right where private road goes left.
	2.2	After stop sign, continue straight through 4-way intersection. Watch for fast-moving trucks crossing on private mine road.
	2.4	Stay right where private road goes left.
	3.1	Follow fence along evaporation ponds.
	5.4	Leave private property of salt mine company and enter public lands.
02	6.0	*N38° 28.29′ W109° 41.72′* Continue straight where easy road goes left to overlook around Pyramid Butte.
	6.9	Continue straight as lesser roads branch left then right.
03	8.8	*N38° 27.21′ W109° 43.98′* Pass through fence and, as the road curves right, a wide area on the left goes to Thelma & Louise Point (see photo).
	9.9	Road curves right and crosses a wide shelf with a scary cliff on the left (see photo).
	10.8	Overlook of Goose Neck on left.
	11.5	Last wide spot to turn around.
04	11.6	*N38° 27.78′ W109° 46.28′* Turn around at well-marked boundary to Canyonlands National Park. Non-street-legal vehicles are not allowed in park.
01	23.2	Return to start.

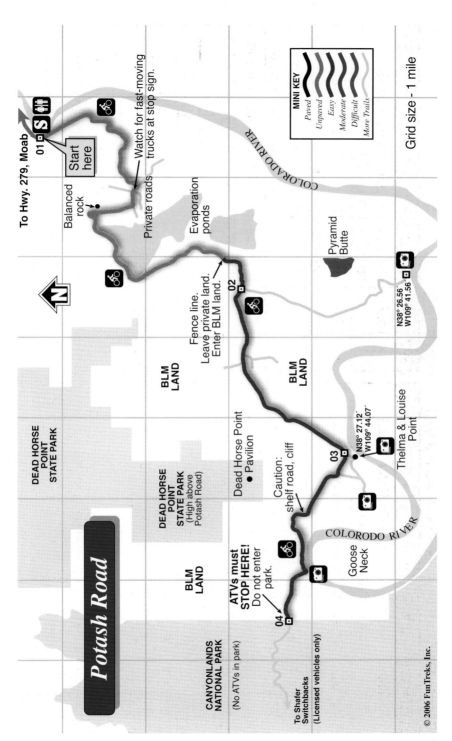

Potash Road

To Hwy. 279, Moab

Start here

Watch for fast-moving trucks at stop sign.

Balanced rock

Private roads

Evaporation ponds

COLORODO RIVER

MINI KEY
Paved
Unpaved
Easy
Moderate
Difficult
More Trails

Grid size - 1 mile

N

01

02

N38° 26.56'
W109° 41.56'

Pyramid Butte

Fence line.
Leave private land.
Enter BLM land.

BLM LAND

BLM LAND

DEAD HORSE POINT STATE PARK

DEAD HORSE POINT STATE PARK
(High above Potash Road)

Dead Horse Point
● Pavilion

Caution:
shelf road, cliff

03

N38° 27.12'
W109° 44.07'

Thelma & Louise Point

COLORODO RIVER

Goose Neck

BLM LAND

ATVs must STOP HERE!
Do not enter park.

04

CANYONLANDS NATIONAL PARK
(No ATVs in park)

To Shafer Switchbacks
(Licensed vehicles only)

© 2006 FunTreks, Inc.

83

Initial descent into Kane Creek Canyon.

See petroglyphs at Birthing Rock.

This shallow crossing can be deep after a rain.

Optional side trip to Jackson Hole.

Shelf road climbs east side of Hurrah Pass. Photo taken from Kane Creek Canyon Rim.

Hurrah Pass

Getting There: From the south side of Moab at the McDonald's Restaurant on Main Street, take Kane Creek Road west. Bear left at first large fork and head south along the river. When pavement ends at 4.7 miles, turn right into the parking lot after cattle guard.

Staging/Camping: Unload at parking lot. Camp along Kane Creek Road after parking lot, but only at designated fee sites. If camping, you can continue on the dirt portion of Kane Creek Road and unload where you camp. Limited spots fill quickly on busy weekends.

Difficulty: Kane Creek Road is a wide, maintained gravel road with tight turns and high cliffs the first couple miles. The climb to Hurrah Pass is a bit rougher but still easy. The west side descent from pass is more susceptible to rock slides and washouts. Kane Creek can swell to dangerously deep levels after a heavy rain storm.

Highlights: A real cruiser the whole family can enjoy. Excellent views from the pass. Stop at the Birthing Rock along Kane Creek Road to see an excellent display of Indian petroglyphs. Close to Moab.

Time & Distance: It's 10.0 miles to Hurrrah Pass and another 2.6 to go down the west side. Allow about an hour one way.

Trail Description: Trail begins at parking lot after pavement ends. You'll descend steeply on a wide gravel road with tight turns, high cliffs and no guardrails. Use caution through this area. The road gradually straightens out to allow higher speeds as you continue south. You'll turn west and follow a steeper road as it winds in and out of unusual rock formations. The west-side descent is slightly more challenging, but very enjoyable.

Other routes nearby: Extend this trip by continuing on to Chicken Corners, Trail #15. For more challenge, try difficult Kane Creek Canyon, Trail #16. You can also take a remote, rocky side trip around Jackson Hole (see map). The first part of this trip crosses sensitive private property. Pass through quietly and stay on main road.

Services: Gas up in Moab. One small, roofless vault toilet at parking lot for Hunter Canyon Hiking Trail.

Directions: *(Shadowed portion of trail is described here.)*

WP	Mile	Action
01	**0.0**	*N38° 31.98 W109° 36.04´* Head south from parking lot on wide dirt road. Use caution descending steep shelf road.
	0.6	Go past parking lot for Amasa Back Mountain Bike Trail. Don't park here.
	1.1	Amasa Back Bike Trail on right, also known as the Cliff Hanger Jeep Trail. (This trail is not recommended for ATVs.)
	1.3	Look for a large boulder on right called the "Birthing Rock." Walk about 70 feet downhill to see Indian petroglyphs.
	3.0	Pass parking lot for Hunter Canyon Hiking Trail on left. Note roofless toilet. Cross Kane Creek and continue south. Designated fee camp sites are marked.
	6.5	Cross Kane Creek again. Water crossings can be deep after a heavy rain.
02	**6.8**	*N38° 27.98´ W109° 36.05´* Turn right following sign to Hurrah Pass. Left goes to difficult Kane Creek Canyon.
03	**10.0**	*N38° 28.93´ W109° 37.51´* Follow winding and sometimes bumpy shelf road to Hurrah Pass.
04	**12.6**	*N38° 28.25´ W109° 38.94´* Follow dramatic, twisting shelf road down other side of pass to fork. Right goes to very rocky Jackson Hole. Left goes to Chicken Corners, Trail #15.
01	**25.2**	Return to start.

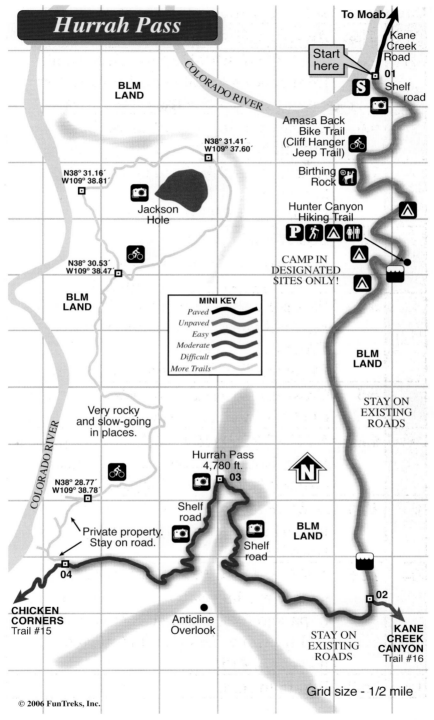

Hurrah Pass

To Moab

Kane Creek Road

Start here

01 Shelf road

COLORADO RIVER

BLM LAND

Amasa Back Bike Trail (Cliff Hanger Jeep Trail)

Birthing Rock

N38° 31.41´ W109° 37.60´

N38° 31.16´ W109° 38.81´

Jackson Hole

Hunter Canyon Hiking Trail

N38° 30.53´ W109° 38.47´

CAMP IN DESIGNATED SITES ONLY!

BLM LAND

BLM LAND

STAY ON EXISTING ROADS

MINI KEY
Paved
Unpaved
Easy
Moderate
Difficult
More Trails

Very rocky and slow-going in places.

Hurrah Pass 4,780 ft.

03

COLORADO RIVER

Shelf road

Shelf road

N38° 28.77´ W109° 38.78´

BLM LAND

Private property. Stay on road.

04

STAY ON EXISTING ROADS

02

CHICKEN CORNERS Trail #15

Anticline Overlook

KANE CREEK CANYON Trail #16

Grid size - 1/2 mile

© 2006 FunTreks, Inc.

87

Ride with a friend. It's a long walk out if you run into trouble.

Crossing Chicken Corners.

Trail skirts cliff edge.

Mountain bikers relax at end of trail.

Hiking trail strictly for daredevils.

Catacomb Rock. Many interconnecting, wind-carved caves.

Chicken Corners

Getting There: From the south side of Moab at the McDonald's Restaurant on Main Street, take Kane Creek Road west. Bear left at first large fork and head south along the Colorado River. When pavement ends at 4.7 miles, turn right into parking lot just after cattle guard. Follow directions for Hurrah Pass, Trail #14, continuing down the west side of pass to fork in bottom of canyon.

Staging/Camping: Unload at parking lot where pavement ends or continue on dirt portion of Kane Creek Road to various parking areas before fork to Hurrah Pass. Camp along Kane Creek Road, but only at designated fee sites.

Difficulty: A few steep sections and small ledges but still rated easy. Not maintained and susceptible to washouts and rock slides. The ledge across Chicken Corners, although quite wide, skirts along cliff edge and may be intimidating to anyone who fears heights. Kane Creek can swell to dangerously deep levels after a heavy rain storm.

Highlights: A remote adventure to two dizzying high points above the Colorado River. See Thelma & Louise Point across river. Explore network of interconnecting, wind-carved caves at Catacomb Rock.

Time & Distance: From start, as described here, trail measures 9.3 miles. Add 12.6 miles for Kane Creek Road and Hurrah Pass. Allow 3 to 4 hours for the entire round trip including Hurrah Pass. With an early start, this trail can be combined with Kane Creek Canyon, Trail #16, and done in one long day.

Trail Description: Trail passes through narrow canyon, then exits up a steep, rocky hill. From there, most of trail is fairly level, crossing mix of sand and slickrock ledges. Continue past narrow point at Chicken Corners until trail ends at stunning overlook. A daredevil hiking only trail continues after trail ends into Goose Neck area of Colorado River.

Other routes nearby: Kane Creek Canyon, Trail #16. Side trip to Jackson Hole (see map for Hurrah Pass).

Services: Gas up in Moab. One small, roofless pit toilet at parking lot for Hunter Canyon Hiking Trail.

Directions: *(Shadowed portion of trail is described here.)*

WP	Mile	Action
01	**0.0**	*N38° 28.25 W109° 38.94´* From narrow canyon, bear left at fork where signs indicate private property to right. Right also goes to Jackson Hole.
	0.3	Follow canyon to left, then turn right uphill after ledge.
	1.4	Follow trail across flat, sandy wash.
	1.8	Stay right. Road to left is alternate route to Catacomb Rock.
02	**2.0**	*N38° 27.19 W109° 40.10´* Stay right. Road to left is main route to Catacomb Rock and Dripping Spring.
	2.5	Continue straight where dead-end road goes right towards river.

WP	Mile	Action
03	**4.5**	*N38° 25.75 W109° 41.38´* Continue straight across rocky ravine and climb up other side. Left goes through narrow, difficult canyon on way to Lockhart Basin.
04	**7.8**	*N38° 27.03 W109° 42.96´* Follow trail as it curves left along edge of Chicken Corners.
05	**9.3**	*N38° 26.50 W109° 44.19´* Continue straight across open area after Chicken Corners until trail heads downhill and ends. Turn around and return the way you came. Note hiking trail that continues around narrow point.

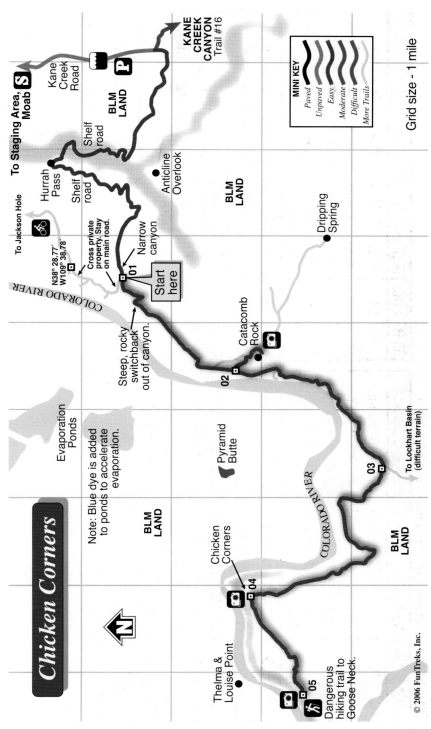

Chicken Corners

N

Note: Blue dye is added to ponds to accelerate evaporation.

Evaporation Ponds

To Staging Area, Moab **S**

Kane Creek Road

P

BLM LAND

KANE CREEK CANYON Trail #16

To Jackson Hole

N38° 28.77′ W109° 38.78

Cross private property. Stay on main road.

COLORADO RIVER

Hurrah Pass

Shelf road

Shelf road

Narrow canyon

01

Start here

Steep, rocky switchback out of canyon.

Anticline Overlook

BLM LAND

Dripping Spring

Catacomb Rock

02

Pyramid Butte

COLORADO RIVER

03

To Lockhart Basin (difficult terrain)

BLM LAND

Chicken Corners

04

Thelma & Louise Point

Dangerous hiking trail to Goose Neck.

05

MINI KEY
- *Paved*
- *Unpaved*
- *Easy*
- *Moderate*
- *Difficult*
- *More Trails*

Grid size - 1 mile

© 2006 FunTreks, Inc.

91

Hurrah Pass Road, Top/Center. Start of Kane Creek Canyon Trail, lower left quadrant.

First crossing after Waypoint 02.

First four miles after Wpt. 02 looks like this.

Watch for deep cuts along edge of trail.

Jeeps go this way. You bear left at this point.

Flowering cacti in spring.

Author hiked to this bridge after Wpt. 05.

Kane Creek Canyon

Getting There: From the south side of Moab at the McDonald's Restaurant on Main Street, take Kane Creek Road west. Bear left at first large fork and head south along the river. When pavement ends at 4.7 miles, turn right into second parking lot after cattle guard.

Staging/Camping: Unload at parking lot where pavement ends or continue on dirt portion of Kane Creek Road to various parking areas before fork to Hurrah Pass. Camp along Kane Creek Road, but only at designated fee sites.

Difficulty: Rocky and washed out in places. More than 20 significant creek crossings, some of which are deep even during dry periods. I found the worst crossing mid-thigh deep. Primary route is sometimes hard to determine through wet section. Easy to get stuck in mud or ensnared in tight brush if you get sidetracked. End of trail climbs rocky shelf road to difficult point where most riders should turn around.

Highlights: Challenging and scenic trip into narrowing, remote canyon with many water crossings. Don't go alone. Stay on main route at all times. This area has been heavily abused by irresponsible riders who think they can go anywhere they see a small path. Trail could be closed if abuses continue.

Time & Distance: As described here, 18.2 miles from staging area to end of trail. First 6.6 miles is easy, maintained road. Allow 5 to 6 hours for entire round trip plus extra time for the unexpected.

Trail Description: After quick cruise on easy road, head into difficult end of Kane Creek Canyon. Cross creek and follow rocky trail south along high creek banks that are partially washed away in places. Trail then drops into creek and crosses it many times. Finally, trail climbs out of creek and climbs steep, rocky shelf road into high-walled canyon. ATV route splits from Jeep route but gets extremely difficult. Most riders should turn around at this point; however, the trail does continue another 2.6 miles to Highway 191. (No ATVs allowed on 191.)

Other routes nearby: Trails #14 and #15.

Services: Roofless pit toilet at Hunter Canyon Hiking Trailhead.

Directions: *(Shadowed portion of trail is described here.)*

WP	Mile	Action
01	**0.0**	*N38° 31.98´ W109° 36.04´* Head south from parking lot on wide dirt road with high cliffs and blind curves. Pass Amasa Back Bike Trail, Hunter Canyon Hiking Trailhead and fee camping spots.
02	**6.6/0.0**	*N38° 27.98´ W109° 36.05´* Turn left at sign for Kane Creek Canyon. When road splits three ways, take first road to left downhill and cross creek. After creek, follow road uphill to right.
	3.7	Bear left and follow bypass around deep ravine.
	4.2	Rocky road follows ledge along creek.
	4.8	Creek crossing begins wet portion of route.
	5.0	Bear left and cross creek at some point. Roads to right eventually end in mud or thicket.
03	**5.5**	*N38° 25.13´ W109° 32.82´* Deepest crossing. Make sure it's not too deep for your ATV.
04	**7.2**	*N38° 23.96´ W109° 32.31´* Pass through opening in fence. This ends swampiest portion of route but more water crossings follow.
	10.2	After sandy whoop-ti-dos, cross creek and climb to higher ground along right side on canyon.
	10.7	Come down off ledge road and cross creek. Pass through stretch where trail follows creek.
	11.4	Leave creek and climb up rocky shelf road on right.
05	**11.6**	*N38° 22.95´ W109° 29.06´* Shelf road rounds a corner and turns right uphill over large boulders and big rock ledges. This is the Jeep route. A small ATV/hiking trail goes left here to a semi-level parking spot. Beyond is a small shelf road that drops steeply downhill to an extremely difficult creek crossing. I recommend most people turn around here, but it is possible to continue another 2.6 miles to Highway 191. Walk down and look at crossing. There's not much room to turn around at the bottom of hill.
01	**36.4**	Return to start.

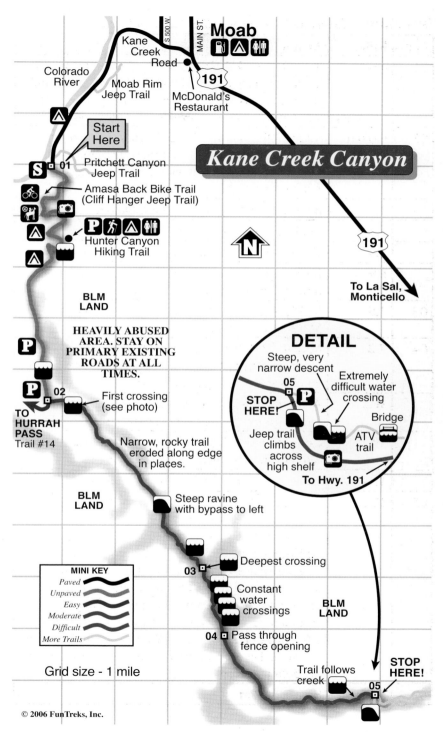

Moab

Kane Creek Road

Colorado River

Moab Rim Jeep Trail

191

McDonald's Restaurant

Kane Creek Canyon

Start Here

S 01 Pritchett Canyon Jeep Trail

Amasa Back Bike Trail (Cliff Hanger Jeep Trail)

P Hunter Canyon Hiking Trail

N

191

To La Sal, Monticello

BLM LAND

HEAVILY ABUSED AREA. STAY ON PRIMARY EXISTING ROADS AT ALL TIMES.

P

P 02 First crossing (see photo)

TO HURRAH PASS
Trail #14

Narrow, rocky trail eroded along edge in places.

DETAIL

Steep, very narrow descent

Extremely difficult water crossing

05 P

STOP HERE!

Jeep trail climbs across high shelf

Bridge

ATV trail

To Hwy. 191

BLM LAND

Steep ravine with bypass to left

Deepest crossing

03

Constant water crossings

BLM LAND

04 Pass through fence opening

MINI KEY	
Paved	
Unpaved	
Easy	
Moderate	
Difficult	
More Trails	

Grid size - 1 mile

Trail follows creek

STOP HERE!

05

Sand dunes off main road at Waypoint 02. La Sal Mountains in background.

Balcony Arch in Lone Rock.

Picture Frame Arch.

Main road continues many miles west, eventually connecting to Pritchett Canyon.

Picture Frame Arch ⑰

Getting There: Starting at Kane Creek Road and Highway 191 in Moab (at McDonald's Restaurant), drive south 12.4 miles on Highway 191. After a long, steep hill, turn right after mile marker 113 onto a wide dirt road. Drive a short distance past cattle guard.

Staging/Camping: Unload at several parking places along side of road. If you are camping, continue farther down the road and unload at various campsites. To camp anywhere in this area, you are required to carry your own portable toilet. Collecting firewood is not allowed, so bring your own.

Difficulty: A wide, easy road, but rocky and bumpy in places. The loop around Lone Rock is washed out and rutted in spots with a few rock ledges around the back side.

Highlights: This short, easy route introduces you to a popular area with many legal side roads and very diverse terrain. Visit two distinctive arches and ride across small sand dunes. Don't get too far off the main road. Most side roads to the north connect to "Behind the Rocks" Jeep Trail, one of the toughest in Moab.

This is a popular mountain bike area. Please be conscious of your dust and noise. Slow down for bikers and offer water if you have extra. Avoid this trail three days in mid-October, when thousands of bikers flood the area for the 24 Hours of Moab Bike Race. Contact the Moab Travel Council or BLM for exact dates of this event.

Time & Distance: Allow 2 to 3 hours for this 11.7-mile round trip.

Trail Description: Head west on a wide, scenic road to distinctive Lone Rock. On the way, make a short side trip to a small area of sand dunes on state land. Circle around Lone Rock on rougher terrain past two distinctive arches. After visiting Picture Frame Arch, return to start or continue west on scenic main road.

Other routes nearby: See map of Kane Creek Canyon Rim, Trail #18, for other side roads in the area.

Services: Gas up in Moab. No toilets or trash receptacles along route. Pack out everything. Pick up after others whenever possible.

Directions: *(Shadowed portion of trail is described here.)*

WP	Mile	Action
01	**0.0**	*N38° 25.32´ W109° 25.99´* From parking area just inside cattle guard, head north, then west on wide dirt road.
02	**0.3**	*N38° 25.52´ W109° 26.01´* Bear left at major fork. Right goes to very difficult "Behind the Rocks" Jeep Trail. Pass through area with many treed campsites on both sides of road.
	2.3	Cross open valley. In mid-October, a 3-day weekend is set aside for the 24 Hours of Moab Bike Race. Thousands of bikers camp in this valley. Avoid riding this trail at that time.
	3.1	Round a curve and head north. A lesser road goes left here. It leads to a minor overlook of Kane Creek Canyon (see map for Trail #18).
03	**3.2**	*N38° 25.11´ W109° 28.65´* Road goes right to an area of small sand dunes.

WP	Mile	Action
04	**5.1**	*N38° 25.93´ W109° 30.14´* Bear right off main road heading directly toward Lone Rock. Go slow and straddle large ruts in road.
	5.4	Bear right at "T." Note Balcony Arch above. Follow undulating, sandy road around to other side of Lone Rock. Stay left when roads branch right.
05	**5.8**	*N38° 26.31´ W109° 30.12´* Watch for Picture Frame Arch on left. This is a great place for lunch. Take time to look around. You can climb to the arch but it is not easy. Right from this point takes you on Kane Creek Canyon Rim, Trail #18. Continue southwest around Lone Rock over slickrock ledges.
06	**6.3**	*N38° 26.06´ W109° 30.47´* Turn left on main road to return to start. (Many miles of easy scenic roads to right.)
01	**11.7**	Return to start.

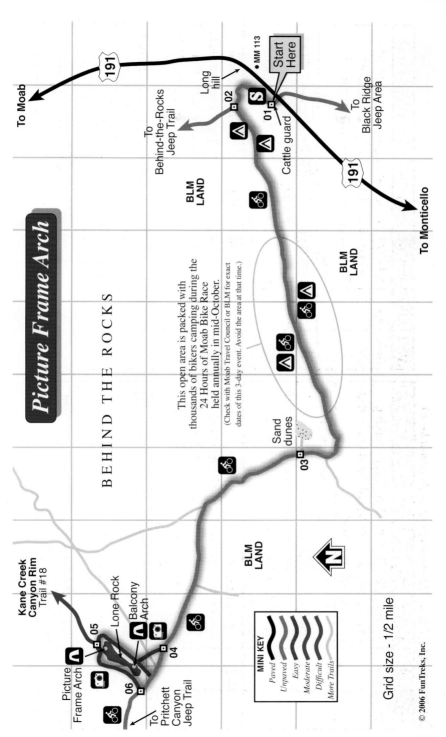

Picture Frame Arch

To Moab

191

191

To Monticello

Start Here
• MM 113

Long hill

To Behind-the-Rocks Jeep Trail

Cattle guard

To Black Ridge Jeep Area

BLM LAND

BLM LAND

BLM LAND

BEHIND THE ROCKS

This open area is packed with thousands of bikers camping during the 24 Hours of Moab Bike Race held annually in mid-October.

(Check with Moab Travel Council or BLM for exact dates of this 3-day event. Avoid the area at that time.)

Sand dunes

01
02
03
04
05
06

Kane Creek Canyon Rim Trail #18

Lone Rock

Balcony Arch

Picture Frame Arch

To Pritchett Canyon Jeep Trail

N

MINI KEY
Paved
Unpaved
Easy
Moderate
Difficult
More Trails

Grid size - 1/2 mile

© 2006 FunTreks, Inc.

Leaving Picture Frame Arch.

Many fun, scenic roads in area.

Take bypass left around steep Hummer Hill.

Inspect ledges when in doubt.

Trail leads to this outstanding overlook of Kane Creek Canyon.

100

Kane Creek Canyon Rim

Getting There: Starting at Kane Creek Road and Highway 191 in Moab (at McDonald's Restaurant), drive south 12.4 miles on Highway 191. After a long, steep hill, turn right after mile marker 113 onto a wide dirt road. Drive in a short distance past cattle guard to park. Follow directions to Picture Frame Arch, Trail #17

Staging/Camping: Unload at several parking places along side of road after cattle guard. If you are camping, continue farther down the road and unload at various campsites. To camp anywhere in this area, you are required to carry your own portable toilet. Collecting firewood is not allowed, so bring your own.

Difficulty: Some of this trail follows segments of "Tip Toe Behind the Rocks" Jeep Trail. This trail has steep, rocky ledges that are difficult for ATVs. Some ledges have bypasses, some do not. For advanced riders only. Don't go alone.

Highlights: Follow difficult but scenic trail to an outstanding overlook of Kane Creek Canyon. Many legal side roads to explore. Stay on existing roads at all times. Watch for bikers. Avoid this area during the 24 Hours of Moab Bike Race, held annually over a 3-day weekend in mid-October. Contact Moab Travel Council or BLM for dates.

Time & Distance: One-way trip described here is 9.1 miles. Add 5.8 miles to reach Picture Frame Arch. You can easily spend 4 to 5 hours by the time you get back to staging area. Add more time for side roads.

Trail Description: Trail heads north from Picture Frame Arch, climbs to a high point, then turns west and zigzags up and down over very rocky terrain. It reconnects and follows main road a short distance, then heads northwest to the edge of Kane Creek Canyon.

Other routes nearby: See map for sampling of other roads in the area. Main road leads to upper end of Pritchett Canyon Jeep Trail. Be careful not to get on difficult parts of "Behind the Rocks" Jeep Trail. It is too steep and dangerous for ATVs.

Services: Gas up in Moab. No toilets or trash receptacles along route. Pack out everything. Pick up after others whenever possible.

Directions: *(Shadowed portion of trail is described here.)*

WP	Mile	Action
01	0.0	*N38° 26.31´ W109° 30.12´* After following directions for Trail #17, you arrive at Picture Frame Arch. Turn right at arch and head downhill over ledges. Road becomes sandy across open area, then gets rocky again.
	1.3	Continue straight at 4-way intersection. Left has nasty ledge.
02	1.9	*N38° 27.67´ W109° 29.90´* Turn left at 4-way intersection. Drop downhill. Trail is rocky with small ledges.
03	3.5	*N38° 26.97´ W109° 31.12´* Turn right uphill at "T."
	3.7	Continue straight up difficult ledge.
	3.9	A steep, black slickrock climb to right is called "Hummer Hill." Bear right but don't go up the hill. Follow bypass ledge around to the left.

WP	Mile	Action
04	4.3	*N38° 27.38´ W109° 31.54´* Bear left. Right goes to a popular extreme Jeep obstacle called "White Knuckle Hill."
	4.5	Continue straight.
	4.7	Continue straight up challenging ledges.
	5.4	Bear right.
	5.7	Stay right where road joins on left.
	6.0	Bear left.
	6.2	Take bypass around big ledge.
05	6.5	*N38° 26.83´ W109° 33.51´* Bear left where road splits just before reaching main road. Turn right on main road.
06	7.4	*N38° 27.55´ W109° 34.00´* Bear left off main road to reach overlook.
07	9.1	*N38° 28.21´ W109° 35.22´* Stay left to reach outstanding overlook of Kane Creek Canyon. Road continues short distance. Return to main road to explore other areas or go back to start.

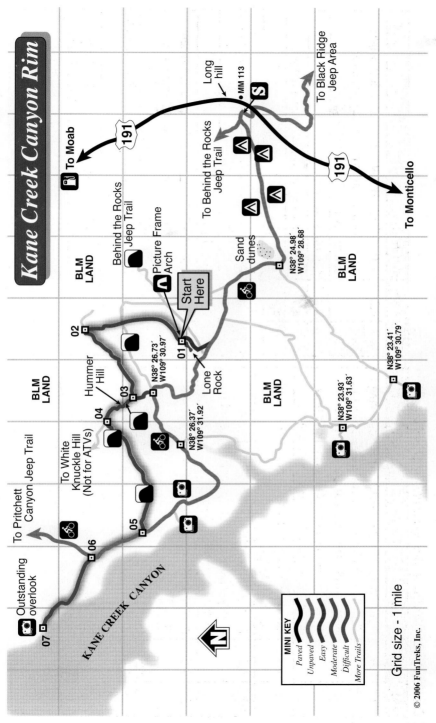

Kane Creek Canyon Rim

Long hill

• MM 113

S

To Black Ridge Jeep Area

191 To Moab

To Behind the Rocks Jeep Trail

191 To Monticello

Behind the Rocks Jeep Trail

Picture Frame Arch

BLM LAND

Start Here

Sand dunes

N38° 24.98'
W109° 28.68'

BLM LAND

02

Hummer Hill

03

04

To White Knuckle Hill (Not for ATVs)

To Pritchett Canyon Jeep Trail

N38° 26.73'
W109° 30.97'

01

Lone Rock

N38° 26.37'
W109° 31.92'

BLM LAND

N38° 23.93'
W109° 31.63'

N38° 23.41'
W109° 30.79'

05

06

Outstanding overlook

07

KANE CREEK CANYON

N

MINI KEY
Paved
Unpaved
Easy
Moderate
Difficult
More Trails

Grid size - 1 mile

© 2006 FunTreks, Inc.

Fun ride on shortcut to Caves Spring north of Waypoint 03.

La Boca Arch.

Explore giant wind caves at Caves Spring.

Old mining camp. Cabins built of old railroad ties have held up well.

Overlook of Professor Valley and Colorado River at Waypoint 06. Great spot for lunch.

Dome Plateau

19

Getting There: From north side of Moab, take Highway 128 northeast along Colorado River about 30 miles to the Dewey Bridge. Jeep entrance to Dome Plateau is on left after bridge. No parking here. ATVs cannot cross Dewey Bridge. Continue another 4.5 miles on Highway 128 to Department of Transportation gravel lot on left. Follow sign for Kokopelli Bike Trail uphill another half mile.

Staging/Camping: Park and unload in open area where lesser road forks to left. Established BLM campground south of Dewey Bridge.

Difficulty: Rocky and steep in places. Novice riders may find some steep ledges challenging. Much of route is easy. Parts of main route can be impassable when wet. Some very difficult side roads.

Highlights: Great riding area with many legal side roads to explore. Very scenic with terrific arches and one outstanding overlook of Colorado River. Explore giant wind caves at Caves Spring (on foot) and an old mining camp with two well-preserved cabins.

Time & Distance: Over 32 miles as described here. Allow 4 to 6 hours.

Trail Description: First part of route follows Kokopelli Bike Trail over very rough and rocky hills. It connects to a sandy, winding road used by Jeeps to enter the area. As a side trip, you can backtrack east on this road to great scenery which includes two arches. One is easy to find, the other is camouflaged against the rocks. Continuing west, you'll drop into a steep-walled canyon and eventually turn south past impressive La Boca Arch. From there, you'll connect to an easy road that heads south to an outstanding overlook (great spot for lunch). When you return from overlook, stay on main road. Roads to northeast are extremely difficult and impassable when wet. The return trip follows a different course past Caves Spring and then through a rocky valley. After passing an old mining camp, a good road returns to start.

Other routes nearby: Trails #20, #21 and #22 are located off Entrada Bluffs Road on south side of Dewey Bridge.

Services: Gas up in Moab. Vault toilet on south side of Dewey Bridge and at Dewey Bridge Recreation Area Campground.

Directions: *(Shadowed portion of trail is described here.)*

WP	Mile	Action
01	0.0	*N38° 51.25′ W109° 18.06′* Stay left on lesser road.
	1.9	Drop downhill through fence, then bear left on Kokopelli Bike Trail. After that, trail becomes rocky.
	2.9	Right at "T." Left goes back to Highway 128.
	3.7/0.0	Bear right. Left goes to overlook.
	0.1	Turn left downhill over rocky ledges (easy to miss).
	0.3	Follow faint tracks across open area of slickrock.
	0.6	Turn hard left at 4-way intersection.
	0.8	Bear left at fork and descend through sandy area.
02	1.4/0.0	*N38° 49.31′ W109° 21.30′* Turn right. Left is Jeep entrance from Highway 128 with two great arches.
	0.2	Stay right down steep ledges and cross canyon.
	1.7	Continue straight. Left goes to difficult area.
03	1.8	*N38° 48.77′ W109° 22.92′* Continue straight at 4-way intersection. Right is shortcut to Caves Spring.
	2.7	Turn left uphill from ravine.
04	4.5	*N38° 47.67′ W109° 24.67′* Bear left. You come back here later and go other way to Caves Spring.
	4.6	Bear right.
	5.0	Turn right to arch.
05	5.1	*N38° 47.44′ W109° 25.07′* Turn around at La Boca Arch. Go back to last fork and continue right.
	5.4	Continue straight on better road that is gated to right.
	7.3	Bear right. Left goes to difficult area.
	9.4	Turn left downhill on lesser road before fence.
	10.5	Continue straight down rocky ledges.
06	9.9	*N38° 44.79′ W109° 22.97′* Park and hike short distance downhill to overlook. Turn around and go back to Waypoint 04.
04	15.3/0.0	Turn left at Waypoint 04.
	0.1	Continue straight. Left dead ends.
07	2.5	*N38° 49.44′ W109° 24.02′* Stop and explore Caves Spring, then continue northeast through rocky valley.
08	4.8	*N38° 49.97′ W109° 23.15′* Turn right at top of hill after rocky climb.
	6.3	Bear left. Right dead ends at overlook.
09	7.0	*N38° 50.30′ W109° 21.95′* Old mining cabins on left.
01	12.2	Continue north on good road back to start.

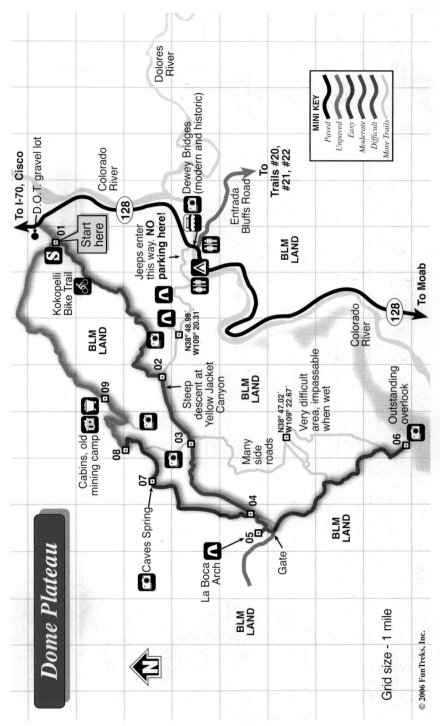

Dome Plateau

N

Grid size - 1 mile

© 2006 FunTreks, Inc.

MINI KEY
Paved
Unpaved
Easy
Moderate
Difficult
More Trails

To I-70, Cisco
D.O.T. gravel lot

01
Start here

Kokopelli Bike Trail

128

Colorado River

Dolores River

Dewey Bridges (modern and historic)

Jeeps enter this way. **NO parking here!**

N38° 48.98'
W109° 20.31'

Entrada Bluffs Road

To Trails #20, #21, #22

BLM LAND

02
Steep descent at Yellow Jacket Canyon

09
Cabins, old mining camp

08

07
Caves Spring

03

05
La Boca Arch

04
Gate

Many side roads

N38° 47.02'
W109° 22.67'
Very difficult area, impassable when wet

BLM LAND

BLM LAND

BLM LAND

06
Outstanding overlook

Colorado River

128

To Moab

Looking down on Colorado River and Highway 128 from Waypoint 07.

Looking west towards Castle Rock from overlook near Waypoint 05.

Climb is rocky and rough.

Alternate way down from Waypoint 03.

Pole Canyon Rim

20

Getting There: From north side of Moab, take Highway 128 northeast along Colorado River about 30 miles to the Dewey Bridge. Turn right just before bridge on Entrada Bluffs Road. Continue east 0.3 miles to parking area on left.

Staging/Camping: Unload at parking area. Camp at Dewey Bridge Recreation Site Campground on left just before the bridge. (Tiny Cowskin Campground on Entrada Bluffs Road is primarily for bikers.)

Difficulty: A rough, rocky road interspersed with sandy stretches. Steep in places. Some side roads have difficult obstacles.

Highlights: A network of fun roads leading to a high ridge with great views of Professor Valley, Richardson Amphitheater and the Dolores River valley. A shorter version of Top of the World, Trail #21, but no less impressive.

Time & Distance: Just under 6 miles one way. Allow 1-1/2 to 2 hours for round trip plus extra time for side trips.

Trail Description: This description takes you up a lightly used two-track route over pounding rocky terrain. It soon connects to a very rough service road to power lines that cross the area. The final leg continues northwest near edge of rim ending at an outstanding overlook. Various side trips take you to other overlooks. On your return trip, you may wish to stay on the main service road all the way to the bottom but be prepared for some rough spots. Stay to the right at Waypoint 03. The road splits several times but all roads eventually reach the bottom.

Other routes nearby: If you continue south on Entrada Bluffs Road, you'll eventually reach Dolores River Overlook, Trail #22. On the way you'll go past the entrance to Top of the World, Trail #21. A major road departs east from Entrada Bluffs Road (see map) into the Dolores Triangle. This trip requires crossing the Dolores River, which is often too deep for ATVs.

Services: Gas up in Moab. Modern vault toilet at beginning of Entrada Bluffs Road by old Dewey Bridge and at BLM Campground on west side of Highway 128.

Directions: *(Shadowed portion of trail is described here.)*

WP	Mile	Action
01	**0.0**	*N38° 48.64 W109° 17.91´* Head south on Entrada Bluffs Road from parking lot.
02	**0.3**	*N38° 48.49 W109° 17.76´* Turn right uphill on two-track trail.
03	**1.4**	*N38° 47.76 W109° 17.56´* After rocky climb, turn right uphill where road joins on left.
	2.6	Stay left at "Y." Road to right is difficult route under power lines.
04	**2.7**	*N38° 46.84 W109° 17.63´* Turn right downhill. Left goes to overlook.
	2.9	Bear left leaving power lines.
	3.6	Bear right over slickrock through trees. Left eventually dead ends.
05	**3.8**	*N38° 46.18´ W109° 18.02´* Turn right at 4-way intersection. Straight goes to overlook.
	4.1	Continue straight. Road that crosses is difficult route under power lines. Left has big ledge before reaching overlook.
06	**4.5**	*N38° 46.54´ W109° 18.63´* Turn left. Follow road through trees as it curves back to the right and continues northwest.
	5.4	Continue straight across slickrock.
	5.7	Bear left at faint fork across open slickrock.
07	**5.9**	*N38° 47.01´ W109° 19.66´* Trail ends at dramatic overlook.
01	**11.8**	Return to start. If you want to continue south on Entrada Bluffs Road, consider taking a shortcut to the right at Wpt. 03. This route has one moderate ledge to descend.

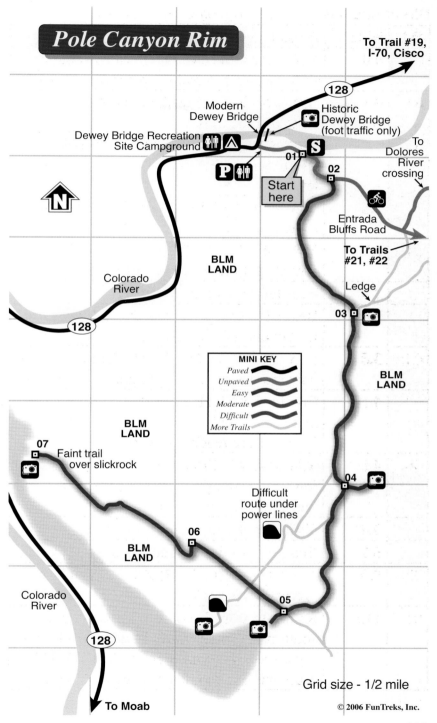

Pole Canyon Rim

To Trail #19, I-70, Cisco

128

Modern Dewey Bridge

Historic Dewey Bridge (foot traffic only)

Dewey Bridge Recreation Site Campground

To Dolores River crossing

01

S

02

Start here

P

Entrada Bluffs Road

To Trails #21, #22

N

BLM LAND

Colorado River

128

Ledge

03

BLM LAND

MINI KEY

Paved
Unpaved
Easy
Moderate
Difficult
More Trails

BLM LAND

07

Faint trail over slickrock

04

Difficult route under power lines

06

BLM LAND

Colorado River

128

05

To Moab

Grid size - 1/2 mile

© 2006 FunTreks, Inc.

111

Looking west from Top of the World towards Fisher Towers.

Turn right here off Entrada Bluffs Road.

Photo does not capture steepness.

Returning down east side of loop.

Southern view from top.

Top of the World

21

Getting There: From north side of Moab, take Highway 128 northeast along Colorado River about 30 miles to the Dewey Bridge. Turn right just before bridge on Entrada Bluffs Road. Continue east 0.3 miles to parking area on left.

Staging/Camping: Unload at parking area. You can also drive another 5 miles on Entrada Bluffs Road to a second parking area at the base of Top of the World Trail. Camping is available at Dewey Bridge Recreation Site Campground just off Highway 128 before Dewey Bridge. (Tiny Cowskin Campground, located on Entrada Bluffs Road is primarily used by bikers.)

Difficulty: First part of route after leaving Entrada Bluffs Road goes from easy to moderate. As you climb higher, rock ledges increase in size and become more difficult. Some of the largest ledges are located on the east side of loop. Be careful along cliff edge at top; there are no handrails.

Highlights: A fun ride with rocky challenges. Dizzying views from high cliff looking down on Fisher Towers Recreation Site, Onion Creek and Castle Valley.

Time & Distance: Entire round trip including Entrada Bluffs Road is 19.3 miles. One-way trip uphill to Top of the World after leaving Entrada Bluffs Road is 4.5 miles. Allow 3 to 4 hours for everything.

Trail Description: Follow wide, easy Entrada Bluffs Road about 5 miles to Top of the World Trailhead (Waypoint 03). Head south past a second parking area. A rocky section is soon encountered after passing through a fence. Stay left to bypass narrow rocky chute. After a sandy stretch, the road steepens with rock ledges increasing in size. Loop can be ridden in either direction. Try it both ways for extra fun.

Other routes nearby: Pole Canyon Rim, Trail #20 is located near start of Entrada Bluffs Road. Continue past Top of the World on Entrada Bluffs Road to Dolores River Overlook, Trail #22.

Services: Modern vault toilet at beginning of Entrada Bluffs Road.

Directions: *(Shadowed portion of trail is described here.)*

WP	Mile	Action
01	**0.0**	*N38° 48.64 W109° 17.91´* Head southeast on Entrada Bluffs Road.
02	**5.0**	*N38° 46.24 W109° 15.01´* Bear right off main road following sign to Top of the World.
03	**5.1/0.0**	*N38° 46.21 W109° 14.94´* Turn right at 4-way intersection. Head south from wide parking area. (East is the Kokopelli Bike Trail also used by Jeeps and ATVs. The trail is extremely narrow with one danger-ous, rocky ledge.)
	0.3	Road forks after fence. Right goes up nar-row, rocky chute. Left is easier.
04	**0.8**	*N38° 45.78 W109° 15.18´* Bear left at major fork.
	1.8	Bear right where lesser road goes left.
	3.2	Ledges become more difficult.
05	**3.4**	*N38° 43.95´ W109° 15.70´* Bear right at start of loop. (You can go either way.)
06	**4.5**	*N38° 43.23´ W109° 15.97´* After a series of increasingly rocky ledges, you reach the top where the trail becomes less obvious. The loop continues to left back down the hill. It becomes better defined as you de-scend.
	5.6	Towards bottom of loop, rock ledges get bigger. Use caution.
05	**5.7**	Return to start of loop. If you liked the ledges, consider riding loop in reverse direction.
01	**14.2**	Return to start.

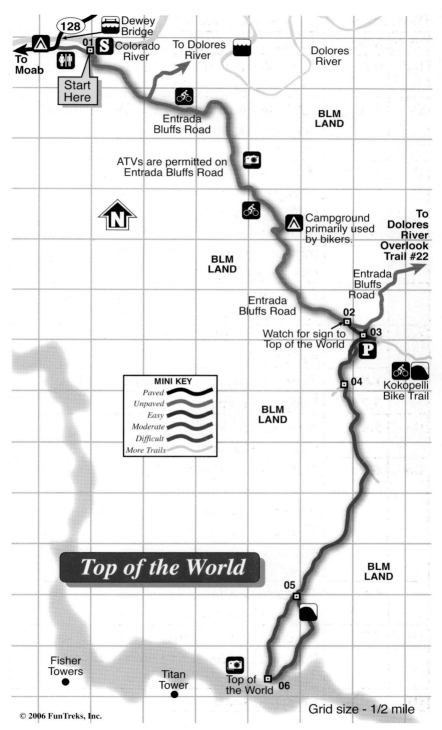

128

Dewey
Bridge

01 **S** Colorado
River

To Dolores
River

Dolores
River

**To
Moab**

Start
Here

Entrada
Bluffs Road

ATVs are permitted on
Entrada Bluffs Road

**BLM
LAND**

Campground
primarily used
by bikers.

N

**To
Dolores
River
Overlook
Trail #22**

Entrada
Bluffs
Road

**BLM
LAND**

Entrada
Bluffs Road

02

Watch for sign to
Top of the World

03

P

04

Kokopelli
Bike Trail

MINI KEY
Paved
Unpaved
Easy
Moderate
Difficult
More Trails

**BLM
LAND**

**BLM
LAND**

Top of the World

05

Fisher
Towers

Titan
Tower

Top of
the World 06

Grid size - 1/2 mile

© 2006 FunTreks, Inc.

115

Descending into Cottonwood Canyon on Entrada Bluffs Road.

Shortcut route at Waypoint 04.

Side trip from Waypoint 06 crosses narrow shelf.

Main route gradually narrows.

End of trail above Dolores River.

Dolores River Overlook㉒

Getting There: From north side of Moab, take Highway 128 northeast along Colorado River about 30 miles to the Dewey Bridge. Turn right just before bridge on Entrada Bluffs Road. Continue east 0.3 miles to large parking area on left.

Staging/Camping: Unload at larger parking area as described above. Don't park in the small area by the toilet next to Highway 128. This area gets very congested, especially on weekends. You can camp in the larger Dewey Bridge Recreation Site Campground on the west side of Highway 128. (Tiny Cowskin Campground on Entrada Bluffs road is primarily used by bikers.)

Difficulty: Primary route described here follows a wide, easy road over gravel and embedded rock. Shortcut at Waypoint 04 and side trip at Waypoint 06 are narrow, rocky roads with moderate challenges.

Highlights: A relaxing scenic cruiser to a beautiful overlook. Add interest and challenge with side trips.

Time & Distance: Just under 18 miles one way. With side trips you can spend at least a half day exploring the area.

Trail Description: First part of trip winds through beautiful canyon along enormous sandstone bluffs. After descending into Cottonwood Canyon, you'll cross a small creek and begin a gradual climb to a high, remote overlook above the Dolores River. At Waypoint 04, you can take an optional shortcut through the trees over a moderately rocky trail. Later, at Waypoint 06, a very interesting side trip goes left. This narrow trail twists along the edge of a steep-wall canyon with great views. There are no major obstacles, but novice riders may be intimidated by cliff edges. Rejoin the main road and turn left to complete the trip to the overlook.

Other routes nearby: To fill an entire day, combine this trip with Pole Canyon Rim, Trail #20, and Top of the World, Trail #21. To fill a weekend, add Dome Plateau, Trail #19.

Services: Gas up in Moab. Vault toilet at beginning of Entrada Bluffs Road.

Directions: (*Shadowed portion of trail is described here.*)

WP	Mile	Action	WP	Mile	Action
01	0.0	*N38° 48.64 W109° 17.91´* Head southeast from parking area on Entrada Bluffs Road.	03	9.2	*N38° 45.84 W109° 13.32´* Continue straight. (Kokopelli Bike Trail goes right downhill through a narrow, rocky canyon. This route is dangerous for ATVs.)
	0.3	Continue straight. Entrance to Pole Canyon Rim Trail on right.	04	11.8	*N38° 44.13 W109° 12.68´* Continue straight. Shortcut goes left.
	0.9	Continue straight. A large road goes left to a deep crossing of the Dolores River. Right is one of several routes up Pole Canyon Rim.		12.4	Stay left at fork.
	3.3	Follow main road as it curves right uphill past tiny biker-oriented campground.	05	13.1	*N38° 43.62 W109° 12.09´* Turn left at 4-way intersection.
				13.5	Continue straight. Shortcut rejoins on left.
02	5.0	*N38° 46.24 W109° 15.01´* Lesser road goes right to Top of the World, Trail #21. Follow main road as it curves left and descends into Cottonwood Canyon.	06	14.5	*N38° 44.59 W109° 11.40´* Continue straight. Side trip goes left.
			07	15.7	*N38° 44.61 W109° 10.28´* Continue straight. Side trip rejoins on left.
	7.1	Stay right where dead-end road goes left. Cross creek and begin climb.	08	17.9	*N38° 44.60 W109° 08.35´* Trail ends at loop at overlook of Dolores River. Return to start on main road.

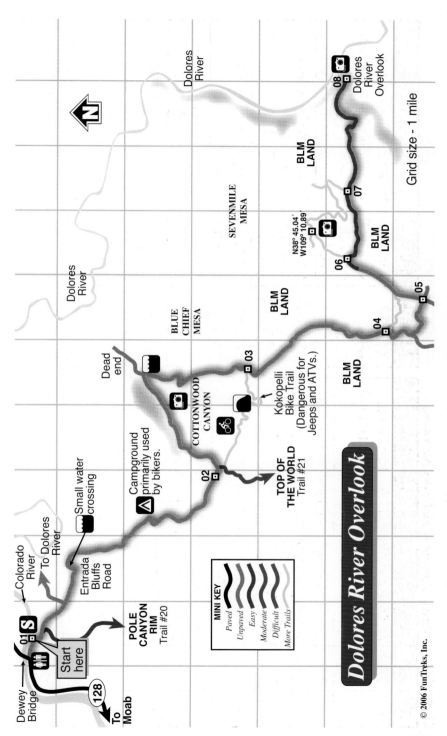

Dolores River Overlook

Grid size - 1 mile

N

MINI KEY
Paved
Unpaved
Easy
Moderate
Difficult
More Trails

Dolores River

Dolores River Overlook
08

BLM LAND

07

BLM LAND

N38° 45.04'
W109° 10.89'

SEVENMILE MESA

06

BLM LAND

05

04

03

BLM LAND

BLUE CHIEF MESA

Dolores River

Dead end

Kokopelli Bike Trail
(Dangerous for Jeeps and ATVs.)

COTTONWOOD CANYON

Campground primarily used by bikers.

02

TOP OF THE WORLD
Trail #21

Small water crossing

To Dolores River

Colorado River

Entrada Bluffs Road

Dewey Bridge

01 S

Start here

POLE CANYON RIM
Trail #20

128

To Moab

© 2006 FunTreks, Inc.

119

Staging area 0.7 miles from Highway 128.

Twenty-seven water crossings.

Easy ride through dramatic canyon.

Slow down around blind curves.

Twisting road climbs out of narrow canyon.

Stop at Rose Garden Hill.

Getting There: From north side of Moab, take Highway 128 northeast along Colorado River. Turn right on Onion Creek Road 0.2 miles after mile marker 20. Continue 0.7 miles to parking area on left.

Staging/Camping: Unload at parking area next to road. If camping, follow signs to Onion Creek Camp, which is a short distance in from parking lot. You can also camp at marked designated camp spots along Onion Creek Road; however, you are required to carry a portable toilet.

Difficulty: Very easy graded road that weaves back and forth across Onion Creek 27 times. The creek is usually shallow, but it can swell quickly after a heavy downpour. Watch your speed. There are many blind curves and cliff edges. You never know what is around the next corner. Slow down for hikers and mountain bikers to avoid a dust cloud. Stop for horseback riders coming towards you and shut off your engine. If approaching from behind, make sure they realize you are approaching, then go around slowly when they are ready.

Highlights: A beautiful canyon to be enjoyed by all. Very popular place to hike, bike and ride horses. A great opportunity to show others that ATV riders can be thoughtful and courteous. Super place to camp and relax. Don't ride in creek except to go straight across on the road.

Time & Distance: Just 9 miles one way to Kokopelli Bike Trail at Waypoint 04. Time varies drastically depending on speed and stops.

Trail Description: Zigzag uphill through picturesque canyon to high point. Turn around and enjoy completely different views coming back down. Those looking to add challenge should go additional 3.3 miles to base of Rose Garden Hill. I don't recommended going up Rose Garden Hill. It is extremely dangerous for ATVs.

Other routes nearby: Short side trip at 0.7 miles goes left to viewpoint of Fisher Towers. At Waypoint 04, left crosses moderately rough terrain to base of Rose Garden Hill. Right takes you over narrow, steep pass to network of popular roads into Thompson Canyon, Polar Mesa and the La Sal Mountains.

Services: Gas up in Moab. Toilet at Onion Creek Campground.

Directions: *(Shadowed portion of trail is described here.)*

WP	Mile	Action
01	0.0	*N38° 43.24 W109° 20.58´* Head southeast from parking area on Onion Creek Road.
	0.2	First of 27 creek crossings.
02	0.7	*N38° 43.05 W109° 19.96´* Continue straight over third water crossing. (A side trip goes left here to a designated camp spot. If you stay right past the camp spot, it leads to an open area with views of Fisher Towers. Once you go past the camp spot, no more camping is allowed.)
	3.0	Continue straight over one-lane bridge. Great views of Onion Creek below.
03	5.5	*N38° 41.90 W109° 16.50´* Trail passes through low, wet area. Let your nose help you find Stinking Spring. Natural sulphur smell lives up to its name.

WP	Mile	Action
	6.7	Small camp spot on right as you leave Colorado River Way Recreation Area.
	8.2	Seasonal gate. If you have no interest in continuing on other roads shown on map, turn around here.
04	9.0	*N38° 41.34 W109° 13.23´* Road gets bumpier and can be muddy. Turn left to see Rose Garden Hill, another 3.3 miles over enjoyable but moderately rough terrain. Right goes to Hideout Campground and Thompson Canyon. Make sure you turn left after another mile to avoid entering Taylor Ranch. (Hideout Campground is very popular with mountain bikers riding the Kokopelli Bike Trail.)
01	18.0	Return to start.

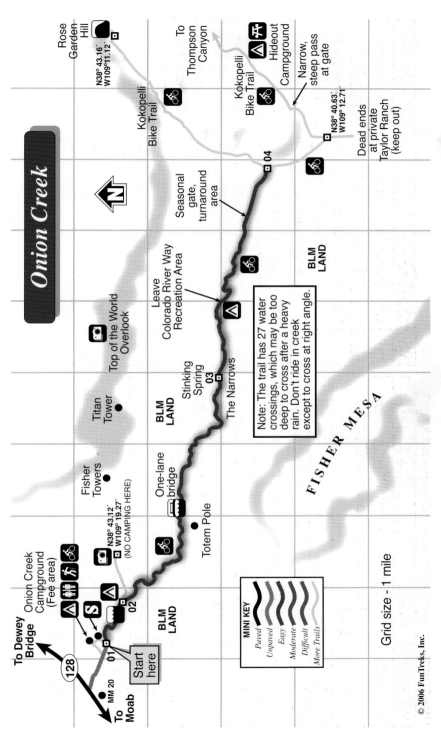

Onion Creek

N ←

Rose Garden Hill
N38° 43.16'
W109°11.12'

To Thompson Canyon

Kokopelli Bike Trail 🚲

Kokopelli Bike Trail 🚲

Hideout Campground 🏕️ ⛺

Narrow, steep pass at gate

N38° 40.63'
W109° 12.71'

04

Dead ends at private Taylor Ranch (keep out) 🚲

Seasonal gate, turnaround area

Leave Colorado River Way Recreation Area

🚲

⛺

Top of the World Overlook 📷

Titan Tower ●

Stinking Spring
03
The Narrows

BLM LAND

FISHER MESA

Note: The trail has 27 water crossings, which may be too deep to cross after a heavy rain. Don't ride in creek except to cross at right angle.

Fisher Towers ●

N38° 43.12'
W109° 19.27'
(NO CAMPING HERE) 📷 🚲

One-lane bridge 🌉

Totem Pole ●

🚲

To Dewey Bridge ↖

Onion Creek Campground (Fee area)

⛺ 🚻 🏕️ 🚲
⛺ $ 🚐
02

128

01

Start here

MM 20 ●

To Moab ↘

BLM LAND

MINI KEY

~ Paved
~ Unpaved
~ Easy
~ Moderate
~ Difficult
~ More Trails

Grid size - 1 mile

© 2006 FunTreks, Inc.

Southern loop entrance.

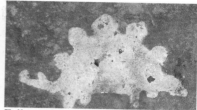
Follow this symbol.

Southern loop not recommended for ATVs.

Giant roller-coaster fins are great fun.

Recommended for advanced riders only.

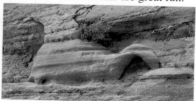
Dinosaur natural rock formation.

Incredibly beautiful area with La Sal Mountains as backdrop.

Getting There: From Main Street and Center Street in Moab, go four blocks east to 400 East Street. Head south to Mill Creek Drive and turn left. Go straight at stop sign at cemetery, then follow Sand Flats Road about 1.7 miles to entrance station to Sand Flats Recreation Area. Entry fee includes great visitor guide with maps. Continue east about 1.4 miles on Sand Flats Road past Slickrock Bike Trail. One quarter mile after pavement ends turn right into signed trailer parking area.

Staging/Camping: Unload at trailer parking area. Continue east on Sand Flats Road to one of two entrances. Entrance to southern loop, just before mile marker 2, is on the right at Campground E, site E7. This entrance is not recommended for ATVs. It is now recommended that ATVs ride just the northern loop, starting at Diving Board Rock farther east on Sand Flats Road on the left just before mile marker 4.

Difficulty: Extremely steep climbs and descents over tire-blackened slickrock. Assistance may be needed at steepest points. For advanced riders only. Make sure you wear a helmet. Easy to get lost. See page 21 for more detailed information on the Sand Flats Recreation Area.

Highlights: A giant sandstone roller coaster with perfect traction, enabling incredibly steep climbs and descents. Absolutely beautiful area.

Time & Distance: Southern loop is 2.4 miles and takes about an hour. Northern loop is 6.2 miles and takes at least 2 to 3 hours.

Trail Description: The southern loop is open to all vehicles but not recommended for ATVs. It is described here because it has long been part of the official Fins & Things Trail. To leave it out would confuse anyone who has previously been on it. This book advises you to follow the recommendations of Sand Flats Recreation Area and ride only the northern loop starting at Diving Board Rock.

Other routes nearby: Located just left of the entrance station to SFRA is spectacular Hell's Revenge 4x4 Trail (not described in this book). It is open to all vehicles but not recommended for ATVs.

Services: Vault toilets at parking lot for Slickrock Bike Trail. Campgrounds have picnic tables, fire rings and vault toilets.

Directions: *(Shadowed portion of trail is described here.)*

WP	Mile	Action
01	0.0	*N38° 34.82´ W109° 29.97´* From Campground E (Site E7), follow signs to Fins & Things southern entrance (Not recommended for ATVs). Follow trail markers along slickrock fins. Fin ends with very steep dropoff then weaves through sandy area.
	1.4	Drop down very steep ledges. No bypasses.
02	1.9	*N38° 34.93´ W109° 29.33´* Turn right at "T" in Campground F. You'll see a steep wall of rock directly ahead. Turn left before wall, then immediately turn left again up rocky trail. Trail winds north then east downhill through Campground H and crosses small ravine.
03	2.4	*N38° 34.87´ W109° 28.89´* Turn right on Sand Flats Road. Watch for traffic.
04	2.9	*N38° 34.61´ W109° 28.56´* Continue east on Sand Flats Road past north entrance for Jeeps on left.
05	3.4/0.0	*N38° 34.60´ W109° 28.11´* Turn sharp left at Diving Board Rock. (This is recommended entrance for ATVs.)
	0.2	Continue straight. Road on left comes in from Jeep entrance. You'll soon cross cattle guard.
06	0.6	*N38° 35.05´ W109° 28.18´* Turn left at "T."
	1.4	Trail descends through narrow, rocky canyon.
	2.0	Continue straight. Overlook to right.
07	2.2	*N38° 35.33´ W109° 29.54´* Follow markings along fin, then swing left downhill to 4-way intersection. Turn right up another fin. Straight goes to Sand Flats Road.
	2.6	Turn right on better road at "T."
08	2.7	*N38° 35.60´ W109° 29.79´* Turn left off better road.
	3.4	Wide area to park next to natural rock formation that looks like dinosaur carved in rock wall.
	4.2	Another big ledge to drop down at end of fin.
	4.5	Follow giant fins west. Great photo opportunity here.
09	4.9	*N38° 35.45´ W109° 30.83´* At bottom of hill, bear right uphill and begin loop.
	5.1	Follow main trail to top of hill then turn back downhill to left. (Note optional steep Kenny's Climb to left.) Follow trail markings downhill. Stay right at bottom over big ledges. Trail goes right then turns left up very steep slickrock hill.
	5.9	Follow trail markers across more fins, then slowly bear right on sandy road.
10	6.2	*N38° 34.96´ W109° 30.44´* Turn right on Sand Flats Road.
	6.4	Return to trailer parking area on left.

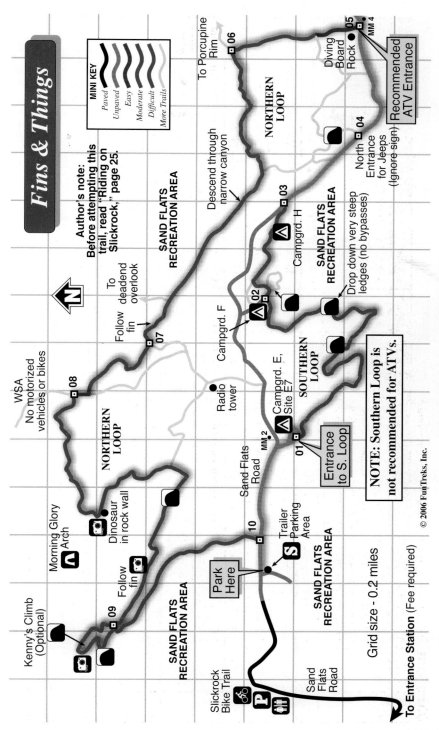

Fins & Things

MINI KEY
- Paved
- Unpaved
- Easy
- Moderate
- Difficult
- More Trails

Author's note:
Before attempting this trail, read "Riding on Slickrock," page 25.

N

To Porcupine Rim

SAND FLATS RECREATION AREA

NORTHERN LOOP

Diving Board Rock

MM 4

Recommended ATV Entrance

North Entrance for Jeeps (Ignore sign)

Descend through narrow canyon

To deadend overlook

Follow fin

07

Campgrd. H

03

Campgrd. F

02

SAND FLATS RECREATION AREA

Drop down very steep ledges (no bypasses)

SOUTHERN LOOP

WSA
No motorized vehicles or bikes

08

NORTHERN LOOP

Morning Glory Arch

Dinosaur in rock wall

Follow fin

Radio tower

Campgrd. E, Site E7

MM 2

Sand Flats Road

01

Entrance to S. Loop

NOTE: Southern Loop is not recommended for ATVs.

Kenny's Climb (Optional)

09

SAND FLATS RECREATION AREA

10

Trailer Parking Area

S

Park Here

Slickrock Bike Trail

P

SAND FLATS RECREATION AREA

Sand Flats Road

Grid size - 0.2 miles

To Entrance Station (Fee required)

© 2006 FunTreks, Inc.

127

Road into canyon is extremely slippery when wet.

Rough in spots.

Travel with friends. Wear a helmet.

Fun, rocky climbs for advanced riders.

Hike to overlooks inside wilderness study area.

Steep in places.

128

Steelbender Loop ◆25◆

Getting There: From McDonald's Restaurant on the south side of Moab, drive 3.6 miles south on Hwy. 191 and turn left on Spanish Trail Road. There's a gas station on this corner. Head east and continue straight through a roundabout onto Westwater Drive. It passes through condos and winds uphill about a mile. Pavement ends before entrance to private residential area. Steelbender is on right just before entrance.

Staging/Camping: Unload across street from start of trail in small parking area. If full, unload and park transport vehicles in larger parking area down the hill. No camping is allowed anywhere in Mill Creek Canyon. Area is heavily patrolled and this rule is strongly enforced.

Difficulty: Steep in places with challenging rock ledges. For advanced riders only. Main road that descends into canyon at switchbacks is very slippery when wet. Under worst conditions, it may be impassable.

Highlights: Gorgeous, popular trail offers plenty of challenge for advanced riders. Stay on marked routes at all times. Trail is surrounded by Mill Creek Canyon Wilderness Study Area. Recommend hiking only in WSA. Start of trail is public road through private land. Future development is likely along this part of trail. Watch out for mountain bikers and hikers.

Time & Distance: Just under 14 miles as described here. Allow at least 3 to 4 hours. Allow extra time for hiking to overlooks.

Trail Description: Descend switchbacks and pass through beautiful Mill Creek Canyon. Cross creek three times on rocky road. After canyon, climb steep ledges, then head southeast along main bike route. Before dangerous Jeep obstacle, turn north uphill and climb to high mesa. Loop around mesa encircled by W.S.A. and descend difficult road with many obstacles. Return through Mill Creek Canyon.

Other routes nearby: You are permitted to ride the entire Steelbender Jeep trail all the way to Ken's Lake; however, a dangerous obstacle after Waypoint 03 stops most people from continuing.

Services: Gas station and convenience store at Highway 191 and Spanish Trail Road. Nothing along trail.

Directions: *(Shadowed portion of trail is described here.)*

WP	Mile	Action
01	0.0	N38° 32.27´ W109° 28.43´ Head northeast on wide rocky road. Trail soon drops down a couple of long switchbacks that are extremely slippery when wet. Head southeast into the trees through high-walled canyon and cross Mill Creek three times over rocky terrain.
	2.2	As you come out of canyon, trail turns left uphill over a series of steep, difficult ledges.
02	2.5	N38° 31.88´ W109° 26.63´ Turn right and begin loop portion of trail. Trail is wide with longer, flatter ledges.
	3.1	Stay right. Lesser road to left.
	3.3	Stay right. Road to left is old wagon route.
03	3.7	N38° 31.50´ W109° 25.59´ Turn left uphill on lesser road. Steelbender Jeep Trail continues straight down a dangerous obstacle. Bikers call this the "Flat Pass" Trail.
	3.9	Continue straight up steep, nasty spot.
	4.9	Continue straight. Road goes right into Mill Creek Canyon Wilderness Study Area to minor overlook. Recommend hiking this short side trip.
04	6.3	N38° 32.77´ W109° 25.69´ Stay left. Faint road goes right to minor overlook.

WP	Mile	Action
	7.8	Continue straight. Left shortcuts to exit route.
05	7.9/0.0	N38° 33.08´ W109° 27.15´ Turn left. (You can hike to best of overlooks straight ahead.)
	0.1	Follow faint road south next to fin.
	0.3	Continue south over rocky terrain along faint road. It curves west and drops into narrow canyon.
06	0.6	N38° 32.79´ W109° 27.08´ Make hard left in bottom of narrow chute and climb up difficult spot.
	1.0	Stay left on easier bypass route. Right goes down extremely difficult Jeep obstacle.
	1.4	Stay left. Bypass rejoins main trail.
	1.5	Stay right. Shortcut goes left.
07	1.8	N38° 32.21´ W109° 26.39´ Difficult obstacle. Left side is easier. Don't get sidetracked on road that goes left here. Trail goes right.
	2.1	Take bypass around right side of big ledge.
02	2.3	Reconnect to start of loop. Turn right downhill over difficult ledges and go back out canyon.
01	6.0	Return to start.

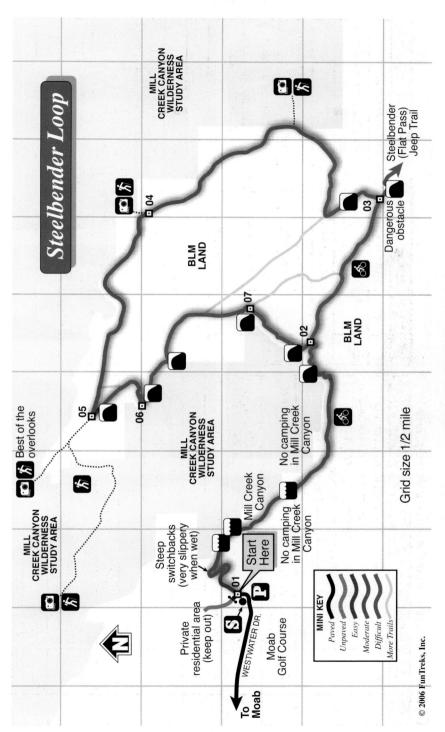

Steelbender Loop

MILL CREEK CANYON WILDERNESS STUDY AREA

MILL CREEK CANYON WILDERNESS STUDY AREA

BLM LAND

BLM LAND

Steelbender (Flat Pass) Jeep Trail

Dangerous obstacle

Best of the overlooks

MILL CREEK CANYON WILDERNESS STUDY AREA

MILL CREEK CANYON WILDERNESS STUDY AREA

Steep switchbacks (very slippery when wet)

Mill Creek Canyon

No camping in Mill Creek Canyon

No camping in Mill Creek Canyon

Private residential area (keep out)

Start Here

P

S

WESTWATER DR.

Moab Golf Course

To Moab

MINI KEY

Paved
Unpaved
Easy
Moderate
Difficult
More Trails

Grid size 1/2 mile

© 2006 FunTreks, Inc.

131

Small staging area near toilet.

Rocky, steep and narrow in places.

Don't disturb wildlife.

Fall color on October 7.

Upper route crosses this talus slope.

La Sal Pass with view of Mt. Peale. Road is easier going down the east side.

La Sal Pass

26

Getting There: Head south on Highway 191 from Moab. About 7 miles south of town turn left, following signs for the La Sal Mountain Loop Road at mile marker 118. Pass by a gravel operation and turn right on Spanish Valley Drive. Stay on this paved road 4.8 miles and turn right on Pack Creek Road which becomes F.S. 73. The pavement ends at the Pack Creek Recreation Area in 2.7 miles.

Staging/Camping: Go past turnoff for picnic area to vault toilet. Unload at this small parking area. Dispersed camping along route.

Difficulty: Narrow and rocky in places. Other places may be slippery and muddy when wet. Snow can block route in late spring and early fall. Not many markers along route.

Highlights: Good summer trip when Moab is hot. Allow time for road to dry out in the spring. Great fall color. I rode this route when it was partly snow covered and was not able to go on many side roads. I was told later that most riders go right at Waypoint 04 to bypass an area where snow lingers.

Time & Distance: Approximately 9 miles to La Sal Pass. Allow about 2 hours one way. (Author's note: For this route only, mileages were based on GPS readings and not the ATV odometer. The turning points for some side roads were estimated from map measurements. All mileages should be considered approximate.)

Route Description: Road climbs quickly over steep, rocky terrain. Narrow in places because of overgrown brush. Upper portion of route has great views when trees open up, especially in the fall. See 12,721-ft. Mt. Peale at La Sal Pass. I was told that the side road on right after Waypoint 05 goes to overlook. It was muddy and partially blocked by snow when I was there in early October, so I didn't ride it.

Other routes nearby: Several interesting side roads to explore. Main route continues all the way down other side of mountain, where a network of roads connects to Geyser Pass or Highway 46.

Services: Gas up in Moab. Picnic area and vault toilet at start. Nothing on route.

Directions: *(Shadowed portion of trail is described here.)*

WP	Mile	Action
01	0.0	*N38° 26.05 W109° 20.35´* Head east from small parking area next to toilet and immediately bear left.
	0.7	Stay left. Right goes to private property.
	1.2	Continue straight up steepening road. Good road joins on right.
02	4.1	*N38° 26.82 W109° 18.13´* Continue straight uphill where F.S. 695 goes left. This road connects to a network of confusing forest roads. I was told you can reach Geyser Pass this way.
03	5.4	*N38° 26.28 W109° 17.25´* Stay right where Squaw Spring Hiking Trail goes left.
04	5.9	*N38° 25.97 W109° 16.96´* I went left here. Right bypasses rocky talus slopes and a spot that can be blocked by snow in the spring.
WP	Mile	Action
	6.7	Cross talus slope, then route turns sharply right at small creek.
05	7.3	*N38° 25.66 W109° 16.70´* Hard left uphill. Alternate route comes uphill and rejoins main route.
	7.4	Stay left. I was told that road to right goes to overlook.
06	9.1	*N38° 25.14 W109° 15.10´* La Sal Pass. Continue straight. Road improves.
	9.5	Continue straight. Road to right goes to Medicine Lakes. Good place to camp.
07	10.3	*N38° 25.28 W109° 14.02´* Left goes to Beaver Lake. You can continue on good road or turn around.

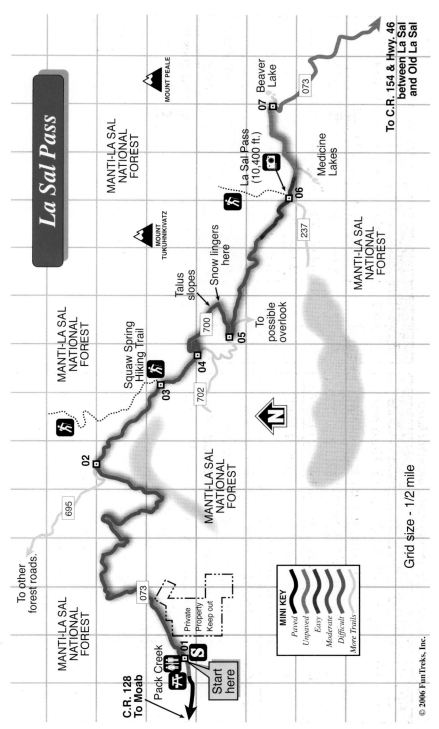

La Sal Pass

MOUNT PEALE

MANTI-LA SAL NATIONAL FOREST

MOUNT TUKUHNIKIVATZ

MANTI-LA SAL NATIONAL FOREST

Squaw Spring Hiking Trail

Talus slopes

Snow lingers here

La Sal Pass (10,400 ft.)

Beaver Lake

07

Medicine Lakes

06

073

237

To possible overlook

05

700

04

702

03

02

695

MANTI-LA SAL NATIONAL FOREST

MANTI-LA SAL NATIONAL FOREST

To other forest roads.

073

Private Property Keep out

Pack Creek

01

S

C.R. 128 To Moab

Start here

To C.R. 154 & Hwy. 46 between La Sal and Old La Sal

MANTI-LA SAL NATIONAL FOREST

MINI KEY
Paved
Unpaved
Easy
Moderate
Difficult
More Trails

Grid size - 1/2 mile

© 2006 FunTreks, Inc.

Dispersed camping at staging area.

Snow blocked route in April.

First half of route follows primary forest road.

Private property, keep out.

Early washout was repaired.

Other roads west of Hideout Mesa.

Final overlook from Hideout Mesa.

Hideout Mesa

27

Getting There: From McDonald's Restaurant in Moab, head south on Highway 191 about 22 miles. Turn left on Highway 46 and go east 16.1 miles. Turn left just after mile marker 16 on Buckeye Road, C.R. 125. Road heads north, then east, then north again. After 1.2 miles, turn right on Hang Dog Road 712 following signs to Buckeye Reservoir. (This road gets very muddy when wet.) After another 0.7 miles, pull over on the right into a small grassy clearing under the trees.

Staging/Camping: Unload at grassy clearing. Dispersed camping allowed along route. Staging area is good camping spot.

Difficulty: First half of route is easy but fun. Don't go too early in the spring. I first tried this route in mid April but had to turn around because of deep snow and a washed-out section. I went back five weeks later and everything was repaired and clear. Second half of route is narrow, rough and steep in spots.

Highlights: A remote, fun area that few people know about. Climbs to beautiful overlook at south end of Hideout Mesa. Cool in summer.

Time & Distance: A little more than 10 miles to overlook. Allow about 1-1/2 hours to get there. It's easy to spend a day exploring other roads in the area.

Route Description: Primary forest road drops into Pole Spring Canyon, then continues north. Watch for wildlife. A large herd of elk crossed the road in front of me before I could get my camera out. After 6.4 miles, you leave the primary road and head south up a narrow, twisting road to the top of Hideout Mesa. Many roads branch away along the mesa, but if you continue south, you'll reach a great overlook.

Other routes nearby: Map shows sampling of other roads in area. Most are poorly marked and some have difficult spots. You can also ride east into Colorado. Two roads shown on map as heading to Colorado state line actually connect in wide loop.

Services: Small town of La Sal, about 9 miles east of Highway 191 on Highway 46, has single gas pump and small convenience store. Look for U.S. Post Office. No toilets along route.

Directions: *(Shadowed portion of trail is described here.)*

WP	Mile	Action
01	0.0	*N38° 20.68 W109° 07.84´* Head east from staging area and immediately stay left on good road (F.S. 777 goes right). In about a mile, the road drops downhill into Pole Spring Canyon and crosses Twomile Creek. Stay on main road as it swings right uphill after creek.
	3.3	Enter old burn area.
	3.6	Continue straight at spot prone to early season washouts (see photo).
	4.6	Road turns left at switchback and descends hill. A photogenic cabin can be seen in valley to right.
02	5.0	Continue straight. Faint road goes right to cabin on private property. Stay out.
	6.4	*N38° 22.98 W109° 05.05´* Turn right on lesser two-track road.
03	7.3	*N38° 22.30 W109° 05.29´* Bear left. Right goes around base of Hideout Mesa. This way is difficult in spots, but fun.
04	8.4	*N38° 21.51 W109° 04.68´* Stay to right.
05	8.8	*N38° 21.21 W109° 04.50´* Bear right on F.S. 805.
	9.1	Bear left.
	9.2	Stay left on better road.
	9.6	Stay left (almost straight).
	9.9	Stay left downhill.
	10.1	Stay right.
06	10.2	*N38° 20.30 W109° 04.36´* Turn right uphill. At top of hill, stay left then right until you find overlook.
01	20.4	Return to start.

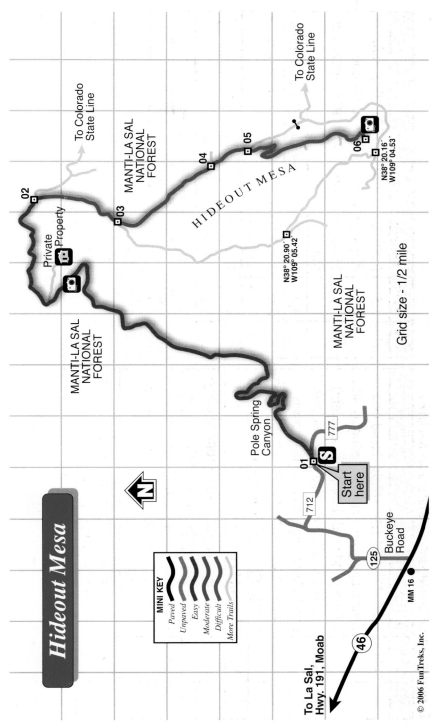

Hideout Mesa

MINI KEY
Paved
Unpaved
Easy
Moderate
Difficult
More Trails

To Colorado State Line

To Colorado State Line

MANTI-LA SAL NATIONAL FOREST

HIDEOUT MESA

N38° 20.16'
W109° 04.53'

N38° 20.90'
W109° 05.42'

MANTI-LA SAL NATIONAL FOREST

Grid size - 1/2 mile

02

Private Property

03

04

05

06

MANTI-LA SAL NATIONAL FOREST

Pole Spring Canyon

777

01

S

Start here

712

Buckeye Road

125

MM 16

46

To La Sal,
Hwy. 191, Moab

N

© 2006 FunTreks, Inc.

139

Steep and washed-out in places.

Road-building may be necessary.

Pick your way through scattered boulders.

Steep, rocky descent into canyon.

Stone cabin at old mine camp.

Be careful across tippy shelf road.

View of Colorado from alternate route.

140

Greasewood Canyon 28

Getting There: From McDonald's Restaurant in Moab, head south on Highway 191 about 22 miles. Turn left on Highway 46 and go east 17.5 miles past a small lake on the right. Turn right on Wray Mesa Road and follow gravel road uphill through sparse residential area. Gravel ends after 1.3 miles. From this point, road can get very muddy when wet. After 2.3 miles from Highway 46, watch for a small road on the right. Turn here into an open grassy area.

Staging/Camping: Unload in open grassy area. Camp here or along trail. Look for stone fire rings built by previous campers.

Difficulty: Old mining road with loose boulders and soft soils. Very steep and rocky in places. Prone to washouts and rock slides. Don't go alone. For advanced riders only. Ride in dry weather only.

Highlights: A remote, harsh area visited by few. Appealing to sportsmen looking for a rugged challenge. Ends at interesting mining camp with round stone cabin.

Time & Distance: As described here, 13.7 miles to stone cabin. Allow 3 to 5 hours for round trip plus additional time to explore side roads.

Trail Description: Follow wide dirt road east then turn south. Road gradually narrows and zigzags downhill through badly washed-out area. Road-building and boulder removal may be necessary to get through. After 7 miles, turn south on what first appears to be a better road. It quickly deteriorates as it drops into steep, rocky canyon then climbs out other side on narrow shelf road. Finally, you descend into Greasewood Canyon, cross Coyote Wash and climb to an old mining camp on side of hill.

Other routes nearby: The area is covered with old abandoned mining roads, many that head into Colorado. A rough road heads south from staging area into Spring Canyon and connects to a network of unmarked roads in bear-hunting country.

Services: Small town of La Sal, about 9 miles east of Highway 191 on Highway 46, has single gas pump and small convenience store. Look for U.S. Post Office. No toilets on trail.

Directions: *(Shadowed portion of trail is described here.)*

WP	Mile	Action
01	**0.0**	*N38° 18.48 W109° 05.89´* Head east on Wray Mesa Road.
02	**1.5**	*N38° 17.80 W109° 04.59´* Turn right at major fork.
	1.8	Bear right.
	3.3	Stay left on better road.
	3.4	Turn left uphill.
	4.0	Continue downhill on narrow, washed-out trail. Be ready for surprises.
	4.2	Stay to right. Don't cross dry creek.
03	**7.0/0.0**	*N38° 14.80´ W109° 03.59´* Turn right. Left is easier, alternate way out.
	0.3	Stay right downhill where roads merge.
	1.3	Turn right at "T."
	1.6	Trail drops steeply into rocky canyon, then climbs out. Use extreme caution.
	4.5	Drop into bottom of Greasewood Canyon and cross Coyote Wash.
04	**6.5**	*N38° 11.17´ W109° 03.42´* Turn left across canyon and climb hill. Stay left when road forks to right downhill. (Right continues south on very rough trail and eventually connects to paved Lisbon Valley Road.)
05	**6.7**	*N38° 11.07´ W109° 03.34´* Arrive at old mining camp with partial stone cabin and collapsed wooden cabin. Return the way you came. (Consider easier alternate route to right when you reach Waypoint 03.)

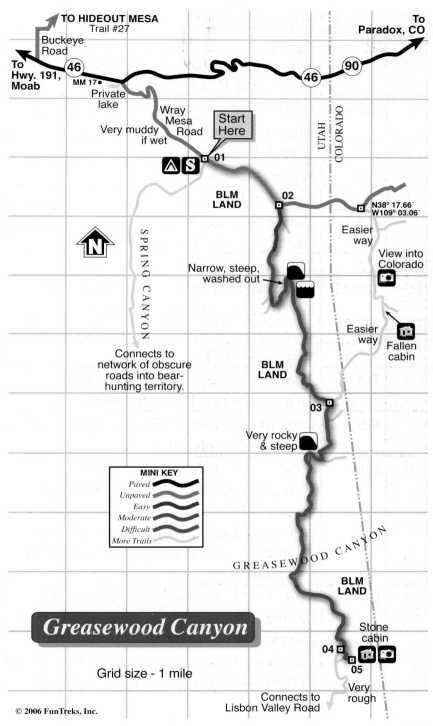

TO HIDEOUT MESA
Trail #27

Buckeye
Road

To
Hwy. 191,
Moab

To
Paradox, CO

46

MM 17

90

46

Private
lake

Wray
Mesa
Road

Very muddy
if wet

Start
Here

01

BLM
LAND

02

N38° 17.66′
W109° 03.06′

Easier
way

View into
Colorado

SPRING CANYON

UTAH

COLORADO

Narrow, steep,
washed out

Easier
way

Fallen
cabin

Connects to
network of obscure
roads into bear-
hunting territory.

BLM
LAND

03

Very rocky
& steep

MINI KEY
Paved
Unpaved
Easy
Moderate
Difficult
More Trails

GREASEWOOD CANYON

BLM
LAND

Stone
cabin

Greasewood Canyon

04

05

Grid size - 1 mile

Very
rough

Connects to
Lisbon Valley Road

© 2006 FunTreks, Inc.

143

Follow dashes up slickrock.

View of Abajo Mountains west of Monticello.

Indian Bathtub.

At one point, trail follows cliff edge.

Looking down on Wilson Arch and Highway 191 from final overlook.

144

Cameo Cliffs/Wilson Arch

Getting There: On Highway 191, head south from Moab about 29 miles or north from Monticello about 24 miles. Turn east on County Road 114 at sign for Lisbon Industrial Area. Follow paved road east 1.2 miles and turn left into Hook & Ladder staging area.

Staging/Camping: Unload at well-marked staging area. General rules apply to camping on BLM land (see introduction).

Difficulty: Challenges include one steep section of slickrock, one narrow path along cliff edge and several steep rocky ledges. Not rated difficult, but novice riders will find it challenging.

Highlights: This trail is part of Cameo Cliffs OHV Area—a fun, scenic area with many trails perfect for ATVs. Trail passes interesting Indian Bathtub and ends at dramatic overlook of Wilson Arch. Great views of La Sal and Abajo Mountains.

Time & Distance: One-way trip to overlook is 14.4 miles. Allow 4 to 5 hours for round trip. Easy to spend a full day or weekend exploring the entire area.

Trail Description: From staging area, trail winds east across sandy flat area then climbs intermittent slickrock. White painted dashes help guide you. A long straightaway passes below tall cliffs before turning northwest away from difficult terrain. You'll then turn north and climb a steep slickrock hill (not as difficult as it first appears), then head northeast along a scenic ridge. The trail narrows along cliff edge before reaching a better road. (Make sure you take side trip left at Waypoint 06 to see Indian Bathtub.) After leaving good road, trail becomes very rocky with several side trips to lesser overlooks. Final leg descends rough terrain to outstanding overlook of Wilson Arch.

Other routes nearby: Trail #30 covers difficult routes inside the Cameo Cliffs OHV Area. A special map (posted on kiosk at staging area) is available at visitor center in Monticello. This map numbers key intersections that are posted on trails. Don't confuse these intersection numbers with waypoints.

Services: Gas and services in Moab and Monticello. No toilets on trail.

Directions: *(Shadowed portion of trail is described here.)*

WP	Mile	Action
01	**0.0**	*N38° 11.38 W109° 21.50´* Head east on trail.
	0.6	Bear right.
02	**0.8**	*N38° 11.46 W109° 20.65´* Turn left, then follow trail uphill as it swings to right.
03	**3.0/0.0**	*N38° 12.81 W109° 19.34´* Bear left. Right goes to difficult Trail #30.
04	**2.0**	*N38° 13.23´ W109° 21.19´* Hard right turn.
	2.3	Bear left.
05	**2.7**	*N38° 13.53´ W109° 21.17´* Follow white painted dashes to right up steep slickrock.
	4.3	Bear right along scenic ledge.
	4.8	Stay right. Left goes to hazardous well.
06	**5.6**	*N38° 15.10´ W109° 19.80´* Continue straight (slightly right) on road with pipe. Short distance to left is Indian Bathtub.
07	**6.4**	*N38° 15.67´ W109° 19.73´* Turn left.
	6.8	Bear left. Cross potential muddy spot.
	7.3	Bear left. Right shortcuts overlook.
	7.6	Stay left.
	7.8	Turn around at overlook.
	8.0	Bear left.
	8.3	Bear left.
08	**8.4**	*N38° 15.57´ W109° 20.71´* Turn right. Straight goes on long, rocky road to Agate Point.
	9.5	Driver's choice. Left is more scenic.
	10.0	Stay left when alternate route rejoins.
	10.7	Continue straight.
	11.1	Drop down steep, rocky ledge. Follow trail across sandy area, then descend to overlook.
09	**11.4**	*N38° 16.08´ W109° 22.22´* Turn around at dramatic overlook of Wilson Arch.

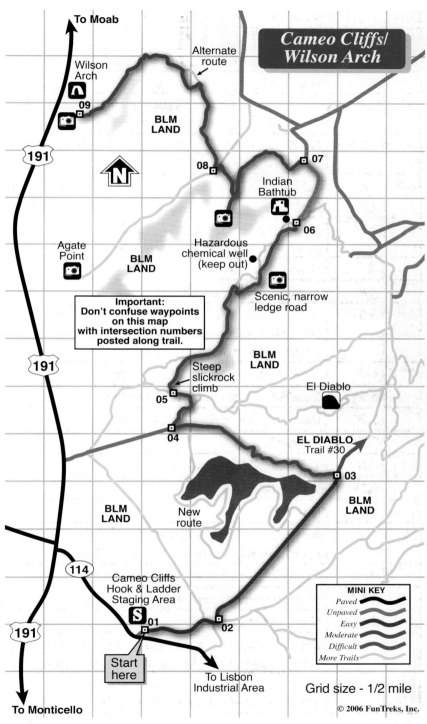

To Moab

Wilson
Arch

Alternate
route

**Cameo Cliffs/
Wilson Arch**

09

BLM
LAND

191

07

N

08

Indian
Bathtub

06

Agate
Point

BLM
LAND

Hazardous
chemical well
(keep out)

**Important:
Don't confuse waypoints
on this map
with intersection numbers
posted along trail.**

Scenic, narrow
ledge road

191

BLM
LAND

Steep
slickrock
climb

El Diablo

05

04

EL DIABLO
Trail #30

03

BLM
LAND

BLM
LAND

New
route

MINI KEY

Paved
Unpaved
Easy
Moderate
Difficult
More Trails

114

Cameo Cliffs
Hook & Ladder
Staging Area

S

01

02

191

Start
here

To Lisbon
Industrial Area

Grid size - 1/2 mile

To Monticello

© 2006 FunTreks, Inc.

147

Lots of room at staging area.

Like a roller-coaster park for ATVs.

Ledges can be tricky.

El Diablo is extremely steep.

Most of slickrock is marked with white painted dashes.

Pass old jalopy near end.

Great views with mountain backdrop.

Crossing dry wash.

148

Cameo Cliffs/El Diablo

Getting There: On Highway 191, head south from Moab about 29 miles or north from Monticello about 24 miles. Turn east on County Road 114 at sign for Lisbon Industrial Area. Follow paved road east 1.2 miles and turn left into Hook & Ladder staging area.

Staging/Camping: Unload at well-marked staging area. General rules apply to camping on BLM land (see introduction).

Difficulty: Extremely steep climbs and descents over slickrock and rocky ledges. For advanced riders only.

Highlights: This trail is part of Cameo Cliffs OHV Area—a fun, scenic area with many trails perfect for ATVs. Route features best difficult terrain, including a steep slickrock climb called El Diablo.

Time & Distance: Complete loop measures 14.7 miles. Allow about 2 hours. Add time to explore many other roads in area.

Trail Description: From staging area, trail winds east across sandy flat area then climbs intermittent slickrock. White painted dashes help guide you. A long straightaway passes below tall cliffs before turning point for Trail #29. You continue straight. After a half mile, you'll descend a short, but very steep hill that begins difficult portion of route.
   You'll soon turn southwest before reaching steep El Diablo. Don't be fooled by the bypass. It is easier at first, but then has a very difficult climb out of the canyon to get back to trail. I found it more interesting and difficult than El Diablo. Go another mile or so downhill then turn hard right and follow rocky trail back uphill. At top, turn right and zigzag back down the mountain and pass through a dry, overgrown wash. The sandy route at the bottom is great fun as it returns to staging area.

Other routes nearby: Trail #29 covers a fun, moderate route to dramatic Wilson Arch. A special map (posted on kiosk at staging area) is available at visitor center in Monticello. This map numbers key intersections that are posted on trails. Don't confuse these intersection numbers with waypoints.

Services: Gas and services in Moab and Monticello. No toilets on trail.

Directions: *(Shadowed portion of trail is described here.)*

WP	Mile	Action
01	0.0	*N38° 11.38 W109° 21.50´ Head east from staging area*
	0.6	Bear right.
02	0.8	*N38° 11.46 W109° 20.65´ Turn left, then follow trail uphill to right.*
03	3.0/0.0	*N38° 12.81 W109° 19.34´ Bear right. Left goes to Wilson Arch, Trail #29.*
	0.5	Continue straight down very steep hill.
04	1.2	*N38° 13.57 W109° 18.84´ Hard left.*
	1.6	Straight climbs steep slickrock (El Diablo). Left is bypass into canyon with difficult climb out (to right) at end.
05	2.0/0.0	*N38° 13.41 W109° 19.57´ Two routes come back together. Continue straight if you went up El Diablo or turn left if you took bypass (a slightly longer route).*
06	1.2/0.0	*N38° 13.38 W109° 20.56´ Hard right.* Follow steep, rocky trail uphill.
07	2.1	*N38° 14.14 W109° 18.75´ Hard right.*
	2.5	Left downhill.
	2.9	Left downhill. Straight to overlook.
	3.3	Trail curves right down steep ledges.
	3.3+	Turn left at "T."
	3.5	Stay right across open slickrock area.
08	3.6	*N38° 13.85 W109° 18.22´ Turn right.* Follow main trail downhill. Ignore lesser branches.
	5.2	Weave through bottom of grassy wash.
09	5.9	*N38° 12.21 W109° 19.03´ Bear right.*
	7.3	Continue straight past dilapidated water tank and old jalopy.
02	7.7	Continue straight.
01	8.5	Return to staging area.

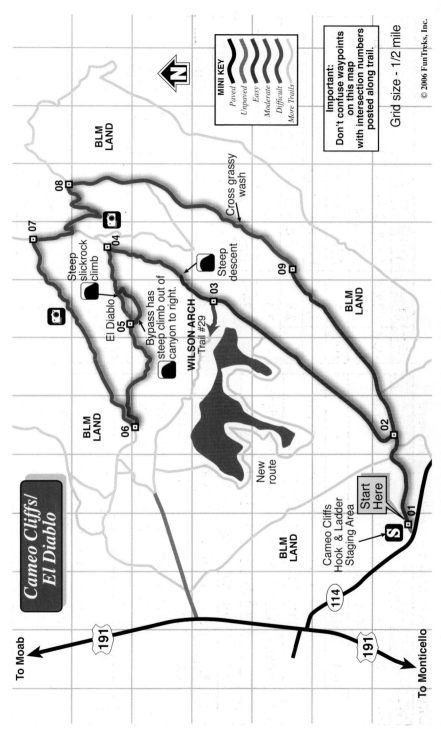

*Cameo Cliffs/
El Diablo*

To Moab

191

To Monticello

191

114

MINI KEY
Paved
Unpaved
Easy
Moderate
Difficult
More Trails

N

Important:
Don't confuse waypoints
on this map
with intersection numbers
posted along trail.

Grid size - 1/2 mile

© 2006 FunTreks, Inc.

BLM LAND

BLM LAND

BLM LAND

BLM LAND

08

07

04

05 El Diablo

06

03

02

09

01

S

Start Here

Cameo Cliffs Hook & Ladder Staging Area

Steep slickrock climb

Bypass has steep climb out of canyon to right.

WILSON ARCH
Trail #29

Steep descent

Cross grassy wash

New route

151

Looking toward Pyramid Butte from Potash Road.

Wildflowers on Onion Creek.

Fall aspens on La Sal Pass.

Moab Rim from an overlook on Poison Spider.

Dirt bikers pose for picture where loop begins on Poison Spider (Waypoint 03).

APPENDIX

RVs set up camp at White Wash Sand Dunes, Trail #2.

References/Maps

ATV Riding, published by Tread Lightly!®, Ogden, UT. Small 24-page booklet with ATV riding tips and minimum impact recommendations. (2003)

Cameo Cliffs, by F.A. & M.M. Barnes, Canyon Country Publications, Moab, UT. Book with photos, history and geology of north and south Cameo Cliffs area. (160 pages, ISBN 0-925685-03-8, 1992)

Classic Moab Utah Trails Recreation Topo Map, by Latitude 40°, Inc., Nederland, CO. Map of biking and OHV routes. (plastic, ISBN 1-879866-22-6, 2005)

Coyote's History of Moab, by Jose Knighton, Compost Press, Moab, UT. A concise, entertaining history of Moab. (1994)

Desert Survival Handbook, by Charles A. Lehman, Primer Publishers, Phoenix, AZ. A basic guide to desert survival. (1996)

GPS Made Easy, by Lawrence Letham, published by The Mountaineers Books, Seattle, WA. Handbook covers the basics of GPS. (ISBN 0898868238, 2003)

A History of Grand County, by Richard A. Firmage, published by Grand County and the Utah State Historical Society. A complete textbook history of Grand County including the town of Moab. (438 pages, 1996)

Moab Country Day Hikes, by Fran & Terby Barnes, Canyon Country Publications, Moab, UT. Forty day hikes around Moab. (1996)

Moab East & West Maps, by Latitude 40°, Inc., Nederland, CO. Two-map set of Moab's backcountry covering biking and OHV routes. (New edition of East map available March 2006. New edition West available 2007.)

Moab North & South Maps, by National Geographic Maps, Evergreen, CO. Two-map set of Moab's backcountry covering biking and OHV routes. (2004)

Sand Flats Recreation Area Visitor Guide by SFRA. Sixteen-page color booklet about the area. Contact Sand Flats Recreation Area, 125 E. Center Street, Moab, UT 84532. Phone: (435) 259-2444

Utah Atlas & Gazetteer, by Delorme Mapping Company, Yarmouth, ME. Oversize 64-page map atlas of entire state of Utah. (Revised annually)

Contact Information

Area Key Contacts

Bureau of Land Management
Moab Field Office
82 East Dogwood
Moab, UT 84532
(435) 259-2100
www.blm.gov/utah/moab

Grand County Sheriff
125 E. Center Street
Moab, UT 84532
(435) 259-8115
For emergencies dial 911

Hospital, Allen Memorial
719 West 400 North
Moab, UT 84532
(435) 259-7191

Manti-La Sal National Forest
Moab Ranger District
62 E. 100 N.
Moab, UT 84532
(435) 259-7155
www.fs.fed.us/r4/mantilasal

Moab Information Center
Main and Center Streets
Moab, UT 84532, (800) 635-6622
www.discovermoab.com

Moab Travel Council
P.O. Box 550, 89 East Center Street
Moab, UT 84532
(435) 259-1370
www.discovermoab.com

Sand Flats Recreation Area
125 East Center Street
Moab, UT 84532, (435) 259- 2444
www.discovermoab.com

ATV Sources, Licensing

Arrowhead Motorsports
2970 Desert Road
Moab, UT 84532, (435) 259-7356
www.arrowheadmotorsports.com

Carbon-Emery Motor Sports
4510 North Highway 6
Helper, UT 84526, (435) 472-8862

Colorado Powersports
(Grand Valley Powersports)
2865 North Avenue
Grand Junction, CO 81501
(970) 263-4600
www.gvpowersports.com

High Point Hummer & ATV Tours
(& ATV Rentals)
281 North Main
Moab, UT 84532, Ph.(435) 259-2972
www.highpointhummer.com

Utah ATV (State) Association
P.O. Box 70586
West Valley City, UT 84170-0586
www.utahatv.com

Utah Divsion of Motor Vehicles
125 E. Center Street
Moab, UT 84532,
(435)-259-1327, (800) 368-8824
www.dmv.utah.gov

Utah State Parks and Recreation,
OHV Education Office
P.O. Box 146001
1594 W. North Temple, Suite 116
Salt Lake City, UT 84114-6001
(800) 648-7433 (OHV-RIDE)
www.stateparks.utah.gov/ohv

Books, Maps (local)

Arches Book Company
78 North Main St.
Moab, UT 84532
(435) 259-0782
www.archesbookcompany.com

Back of Beyond Bookstore
83 N. Main
Moab, UT 84532
(435) 259-5154
www.backofbeyondbooks.com

Canyonlands Natural History Association
3031 South Highway 191
Moab, UT 84532
(435) 259-6003
(800) 840-8978
www.cnha.org

GearHeads Outdoor Store
471 South Main #1
Moab, UT 84532
(435) 259-4327

GPS Sources

Delorme Mapping
P.O. Box 298
Yarmouth, ME 04096
(800) 561-5105
www.delorme.com

Garmin International
1200 E. 151st Street
Olathe, KS 66062
(800) 800-1020
www.garmin.com

National Geographic Maps
P.O. Box 4357
Evergreen, CO 80437
(800) 962-1643
www.nationalgeographic.com/maps

Ram Mounts
(mounts for GPS units)
(206) 763-8361
www.ram-mount.com

Online Information:

www.4x4books.com
GPS products & 4WD books

www.atvsource.com/clubs/state/utah.htm
Listing of Utah ATV clubs and more.

www.atvutah.com
General ATV information for state of Utah

www.discovermoab.com
Moab Travel Council
General information on Moab

www.moabhappenings.com
Latest information on Moab activities. (They also publish a free newspaper available at many locations in Moab.)

www.moab-utah.com/pets
Listing of kennels and veterinarians in Moab.

www.ridewithrespect.org
Single-track trails & Map for Sovereign Trail System

www.thepett.com
Wag Bags®
Portable Environmental Toilet System

www.utahatvtrails.com
Information on Utah ATV trails

RV Parks, Campgrounds

Archview Resort & RV Park
N. Hwy. 191 at 313
Moab, UT 84532
(435) 259-7854, (800) 813-6622
www.archviewresort.com

BLM Campground Information
(435) 259-2100
www.blm.gov/utah/moab

Canyonlands Campground
555 South Main
Moab, UT 84532
(435) 259-6848, (800) 522-6848
www.canyonlandsrv.com

Moab Valley RV Park
1773 N. Hwy. 191
Moab, UT 84532
(435) 259-4469
www.moabvalleyrv.com

Portal RV Park
1261 N. Hwy. 191
Moab, UT 84532
(435) 259-6108, (800) 574-2028
www.portalrvpark.com

Slickrock Campground
1301-1/2 N. Hwy. 191
Moab, UT 84532
(435) 259-7660, (800) 448-8873
www.slickrockcampground.com

Riverside Oasis C.G. & RV Park
1871 North Highway 191
Moab, UT 84532
(435) 259-3424, (877) 285-7757
www.riversideoasis.com

Spanish Trail RV Park
2980 S. Hwy. 191
Moab, UT 84532, (800) 787-2751
www.spanishtrailrvpark.com

Other Helpful Contacts

Arches National Park
P.O. Box 907
Moab, UT 84532
(435) 719-2299
www.nps.gov/arch
(ATVs are not allowed in park.)

Canyonlands By Night
1861 North Highway 191
Moab, UT 84532
(435) 259-2628
www.canyonlandsbynight.com

Canyonlands National Park
2282 SW Resource Road
Moab, UT 84532
(435) 719-2313
www.nps.gov/cany
(ATVs are not allowed in park.)

City Market
425 South Main Street
Moab, UT 84532
(435) 259-5181

Dead Horse Point State Park
P.O. Box 609
Moab, UT 84532
(435) 259-2614
www.stateparks.utah.gov
(No ATV trails in park.)

Maverik Gas Stations in Moab
(For nonresident permits)
435 N. Main, (435) 259-8718
985 S. Hwy. 191, (435) 259-0775

Tread Lightly! Inc.
298 24th Street, Suite 325
Ogden, UT 84401
(800) 966-9900
www.treadlightly.org

About the Author

Charles A. Wells graduated from Ohio State University in 1969 with a degree in graphic design. After practicing design in Ohio, he moved to Colorado Springs in 1980 and worked 18 years in the printing business. Over the years, he and his family enjoyed a wide array of outdoor activities including hiking, biking, rafting and skiing. He bought an SUV in 1994 and immediately got addicted to exploring Colorado's remote backcountry. He later joined a four-wheel-drive club and learned about hardcore four-wheeling.

Dissatisfied with the four-wheel-drive guidebooks on the market, he decided to write his own. His first book on Colorado sold well enough for him to leave his regular job to write full time. He later fell in love with Moab and returned year after year. He presently has six SUV/Jeeping books on the market—two on Colorado, one on Moab, one on Arizona and two on California. More are planned.

He noticed sales of his Jeeping books were increasing at ATV stores with more customers calling to ask which trails allowed ATVs. He began including ATV information in his regular books. Seeing more and more ATVs on the trails, he decided to try it himself and quickly got hooked. He bought his own ATV and began riding more frequently and recently completed all the routes in this book.

This book represents what is hoped to be the first in a series of quality guidebooks for ATV enthusiasts. A new, simpler, full-color format has been designed based on what the author has learned on the trails. Let him know what you think.

Author on Kane Creek Canyon Rim, Trail #18. (Overlook at Waypoint 07.)

Order Form

Order 4 ways: (We accept Visa, Mastercard, Discover, American Express)
1. Call toll-free **1-877-222-7623**
2. Online at www.funtreks.com (secure site)
3. By Mail: Send this completed order form to:
   FunTreks, Inc, P. O. Box 3127, Monument, CO 80132
4. Fax this completed order form to 719-277-7411.

Please send me the following book(s): (I understand that if I am not completely satisfied, I may return the book(s) for a full refund, no questions asked.)

Qty.

ATV Trails Guide, Moab, UT (full color)
ISBN 0-9664976-7-8, 160 pages, Price $18.95 _____

Guide to Moab, UT Backroads & 4-Wheel Drive Trails
ISBN 0-9664976-2-7, 268 pages, Price $24.95 _____

Guide to Colorado Backroads & 4-Wheel Drive Trails (2nd Edition)
ISBN 0-9664976-6-X, 286 pages, Price $24.95 _____

Guide to Colorado Backroads & 4-Wheel Drive Trails, Vol. 2
ISBN 0-9664976-1-9, 172 pages, Price $18.95 _____

Guide to Arizona Backroads & 4-Wheel Drive Trails
ISBN 0-9664976-3-5, 286 pages, Price $24.95 _____

Guide to Southern California Backroads & 4-Wheel Drive Trails
ISBN 0-9664976-4-3, 286 pages, Price $24.95 _____

Guide to Northern California Backroads & 4-Wheel Drive Trails
ISBN 0-9664976-5-1, 286 pages, Price $24.95 _____

Name: (please print)_____

Address:_____

City:_____ State:____ Zip:_____

Telephone: (_____) _____-_____

Sales Tax: Colorado residents add 2.9%. (Subject to change without notice.)
Shipping: $4.00 for first book and $1.00 for each additional book.

Payment Method: Check one:
_____ Check
_____ Visa
_____ Mastercard   Card number:_____
_____ Discover   Expiration Date:_____
_____ American Express   Name on card:_____

Thanks for your order.